THIS BOOK BELONGS TO:

....

....

THE REPAIR SHOP CRAFT BOOK

OVER 30 CREATIVE CRAFTS FOR CHILDREN

ILLUSTRATED BY
SÒNIA ALBERT

First published 2023 by Walker Entertainment
an imprint of Walker Books Ltd
87 Vauxhall Walk, London SE11 5HJ

This edition published 2024

10 9 8 7 6 5 4 3 2 1

Text by Walker Books Ltd

Based on *The Repair Shop*, developed and produced by Ricochet Ltd

This book has been typeset in Caslon Pro

Printed in China

British Library Cataloguing in Publication Data:
a catalogue record for this book is available from the British Library

ISBN 978-1-5295-1885-6

www.walker.co.uk

**All activities are for information and/or entertainment purposes only.
Adult supervision is required for all activities.**

INTRODUCTION

The talented crafters at The Repair Shop restore precious objects using their skill, knowledge and creativity. In this book, you too can step into the world of crafting and learn how to make amazing, classic crafts, with a little help from your favourite repairers along the way.

Crafting is so much fun, and it's even more fun to craft together. Ask an adult to help you work through the illustrated step-by-step guides on each page to bring your crafts to life. Look out for the handy tips throughout this book with ideas to help you be even more creative.

It's important to re-use and upcycle as much as you can when you're crafting and many of the activities in this book use everyday household items, ready to be transformed into treasured objects. Not only is it exciting to bring unused objects back to life, it's also kind to the environment to fix old things rather than buying new. Look out for scraps of used wrapping paper, leftover ribbon or wool and even empty plastic bottles. Keep your crafting treasures in a craft box so that you always have the perfect materials to hand when inspiration strikes.

Turn the page to step inside the magical world of The Repair Shop and begin your crafting adventure!

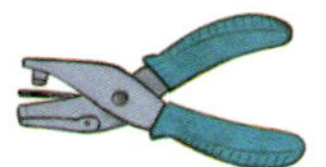  

CONTENTS

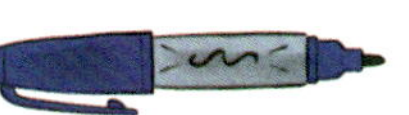  

MAKING TOYS

PERFECT PRESENTS

KIRSTEN MARK STEVE SUZIE BRENTON DAVID

      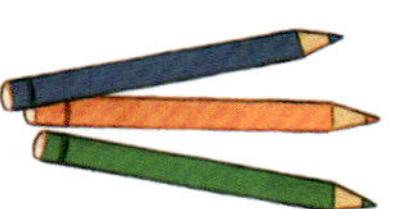

OUTDOOR ACTIVITIES

DO-IT-YOURSELF DECORATIONS

GET CRAFTING!

It's easy to get crafting. All you need is a little inspiration, some step-by-step instructions and a bit of practice. Here are a few things to think about before you get going:

- **Craft together!** It's so much more fun when you have an adult on hand to help – especially with tricky steps like sewing or cutting. They may also have great ideas and advice to make your project even better.
- **Go green!** From old socks, broken buttons or even cardboard toilet rolls, there are so many household items you can collect and re-use for your craft projects. And, even better, you're re-using things instead of throwing them away, which means you're doing your bit for the planet too.
- **Get inspired!** Crafty inspiration can strike at any moment. Keep a notebook with you while you're out and about to jot down any doodles and ideas for more craft projects!

GET COLLECTING!

Lots of everyday materials make amazing crafts. Decorate a leftover cardboard box to make your very own craft box and fill it with a collection of handy bits and bobs. Here are a few ideas for your craft kit:

- **Ribbons:** Lots of clothes have loops of ribbons in to hold them in place on hangers. Ask an adult to snip the ribbons out of the clothes. Keep a lookout for leftover ribbons from presents too.
- **Toilet rolls:** The cardboard tube inside a toilet roll is perfect for so many crafts. From making a pair of binoculars, a simple bird feeder or even a noisy musical instrument – there are so many possibilities for fun with a roll of cardboard and lots of imagination.
- **Wrapping paper:** Keep any used wrapping paper. It can be smoothed out and folded, ready to use in a pretty craft project. Scraps of paper also come in handy for so many craft activities.
- **Dried twigs and leaves:** Natural objects like small twigs and leaves are perfect for stencilling, rubbing or painting crafts. Pick up any pretty leaves you see and bring them home to dry.
- **Beads and buttons:** You never know when a button or bead might be just what you need. Keep any pretty beads and old buttons in a little jar, ready for your next project.

First Craft Skills

In this book, you'll learn how to sew, stick, paint and so much more! Before you get started, here are a few basic skills you'll need:

- **Measuring:** Use a small ruler on paper, card or material and mark measurements with a pencil to make sure your craft projects turn out perfectly. Use a tape measure for longer measurements.

- **Painting:** Poster paint is perfect for crafting as it washes off your hands easily. When you're ready to use a different colour, swirl your paintbrush in a little water and wipe dry with some kitchen towel before applying paint again.

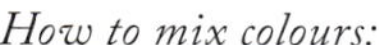

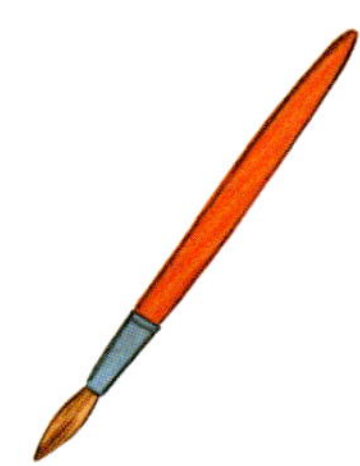

How to mix colours:

1. The primary colours are red, yellow and blue.
2. Select 1 primary colour and mix it with another primary colour (the chart below shows the colour you will get if you mix 2 primary colours together).

3. To make more colours, mix 1 primary and 1 secondary colour (a colour made from 2 primary colours) together.
4. To make your colour lighter, add a little white paint. To make it darker, add a little black paint.

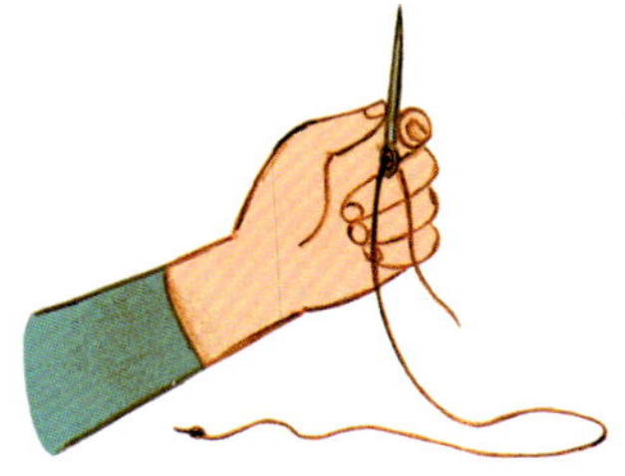

- **Sewing:** Below are simple guides to threading a needle and sewing a running stitch – just make sure there is an adult on hand to help you.

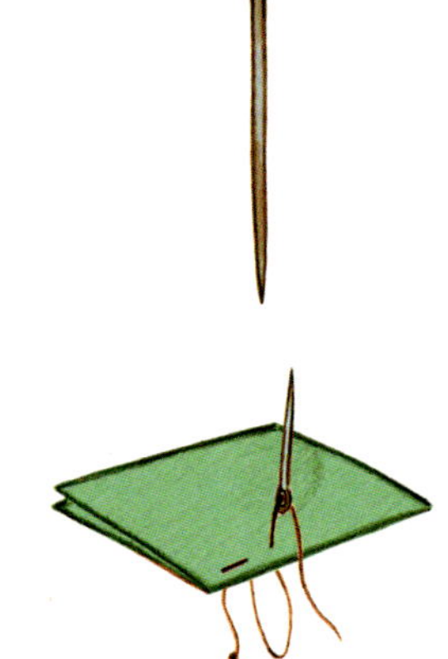

How to thread a needle:

1. Select a needle that has an eye wide enough for your choice of thread.
2. Unravel as much thread as you need and cut the end with scissors. Don't use more than an arm's length of thread to avoid getting in a tangle!
3. Hold the needle between your thumb and forefinger and carefully push one end of the thread through the eye of the needle.
4. Pull at least 10cm of thread through the eye of the needle, then ask an adult to help you tie a little knot in the other end. This will hold the thread in place once you start to sew.

How to sew a running stitch:

1. Carefully poke the needle up through the fabric, then pull it and the thread through (the knot will hold it in place).
2. Poke the needle back down into the fabric (about 0.5cm after the first hole).
3. Pull the thread down through the fabric and you'll have your first stitch.
4. Repeat steps 1–3 until you have lots of stitches, trying to make the length and distance between each stitch as even as you can.
5. When you have finished sewing, ask an adult to help you tie the stitch off.

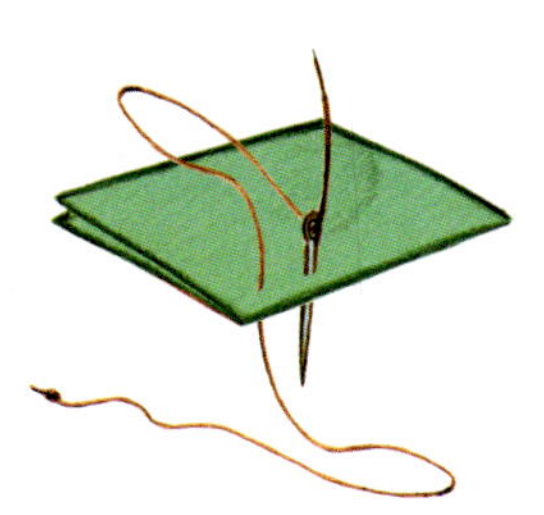

Craft cupboard

Before you get started on a craft project, it's a good idea to check that you have all the equipment you will need. Here is some of the equipment used in this book:

Baking paper

Gardening twine

Paper straws

Safety scissors

Buttons

Glue gun

Pencils

Sewing pins

Card

Hole punch

Poster paints

Colourful tape

Cardboard

Sticky tape

Glue stick

PVA glue

Cardboard toilet rolls

Cotton thread

Modelling clay

Shoeboxes

Tissue paper

Crayons

Newspaper

Paper bowls

Wide-eyed needle

Fabric pen

Paper

Ribbon

Wire coat hangers

Felt

Paintbrush

Ruler

Wool

MAKING TOYS

BUTTON SOCK PUPPETS

YOU WILL NEED:

A ruler

A pencil

1 A5 sheet of pink card

Scissors

1 old sock (adult-sized)

PVA glue

2 buttons

A 70cm length of brightly coloured wool

A short strand of cotton thread

A wide-eyed needle

Ask an adult if they have an odd sock lying around that you can use to make a sock puppet. Stripy or spotty socks make particularly fun puppets.

METHOD:

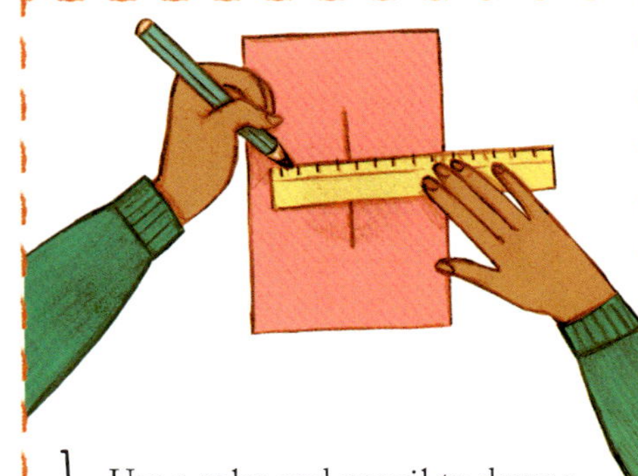

1 Use a ruler and pencil to draw a 6cm line on your sheet of card. Then draw another 6cm line across the first line to make a cross shape.

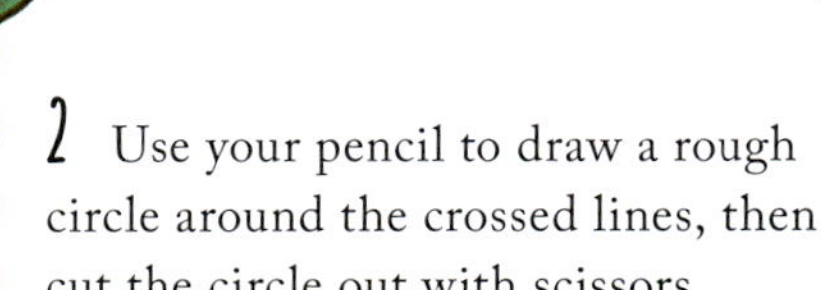

2 Use your pencil to draw a rough circle around the crossed lines, then cut the circle out with scissors.

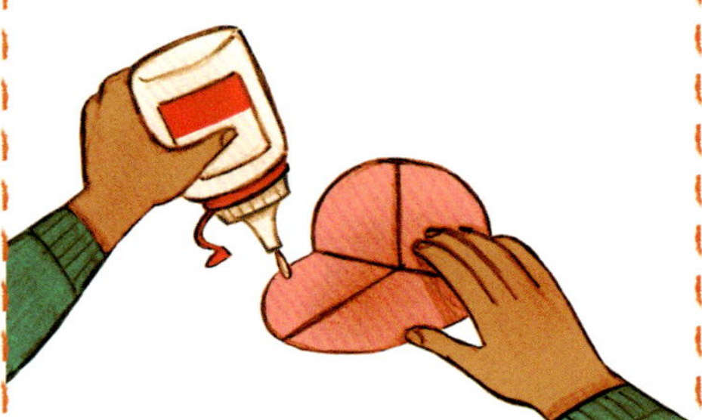

3 Fold the circle in half along one of the lines. Open it back up and spread glue over the crossed-line side.

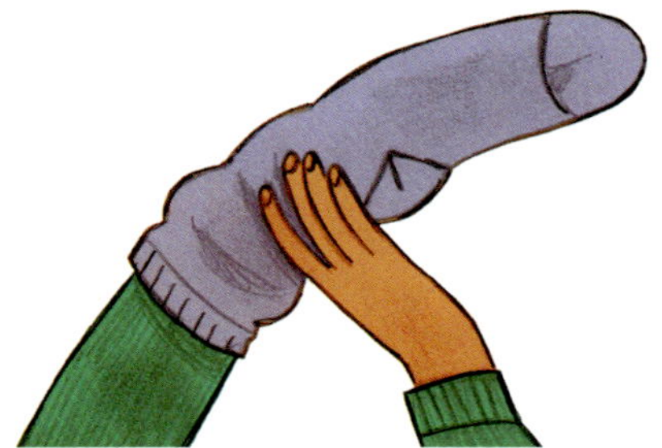

4 Wiggle your hand into the sock until your fingers are in the toe part and your thumb is in the heel part.

5 Use your other hand to press the glued side of the circle onto the space between your fingers and thumb (in the sock).

6 Squeeze your fingers and thumb together, bending the cardboard circle shut so that it is pressed tightly against the fabric. Hold it firmly until the cardboard is stuck to the fabric, then place the sock to one side.

CRAFTY TIP:

If you have any leftover cardboard, cut out little circles and stick them onto your puppet as extra decoration!

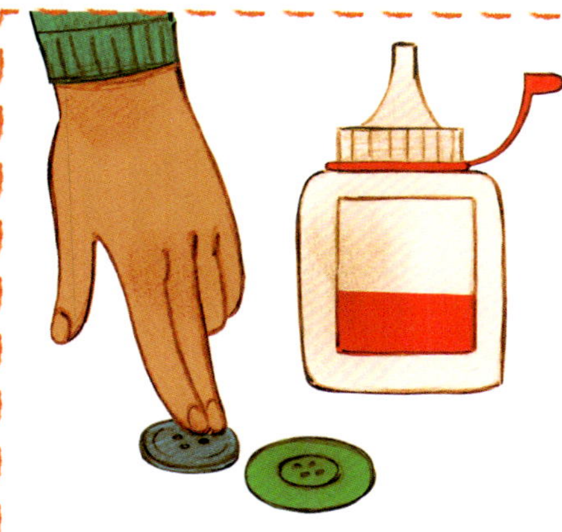

7 Cut 2 little circles out of the remaining card that are roughly the size of your 2 buttons. Stick your buttons onto the card and leave to dry.

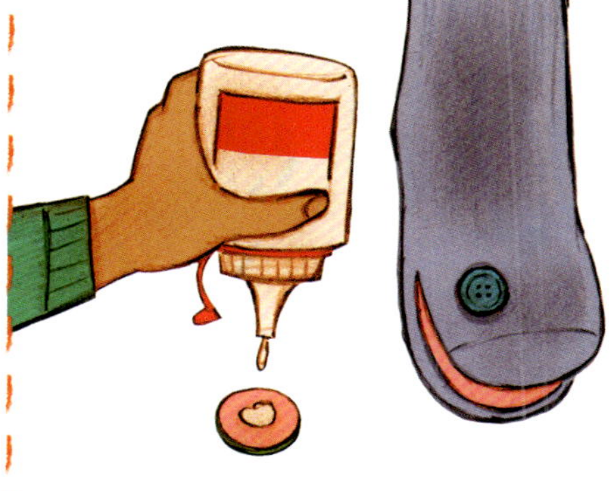

8 Add a little glue to the backs of the cardboard circles and stick them to the top of the sock puppet to make the eyes, then leave to dry.

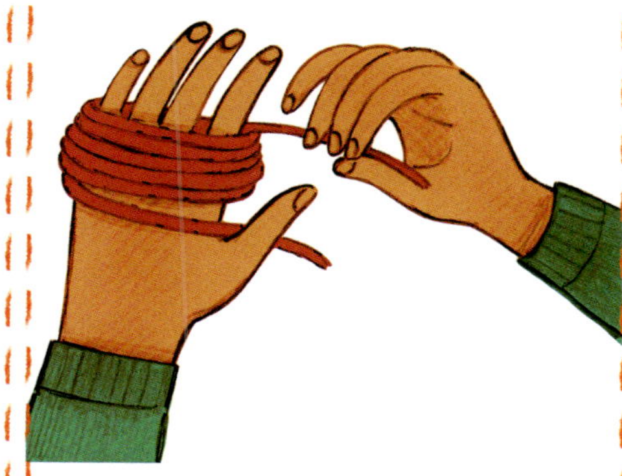

9 To make the hair, cut 10cm off your length of wool and set aside. Wrap the remaining 60cm of wool around your hand until you have 6 equal loops.

10 Take the first piece of wool and use it to tie the 6 loops together around the middle. Use your scissors to cut the loops of wool at the ends.

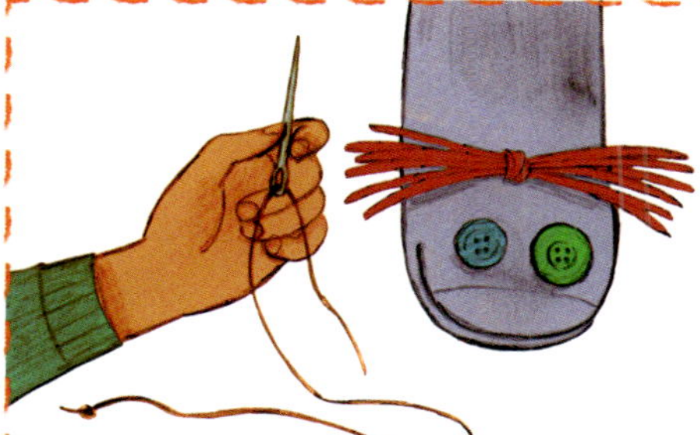

11 Ask an adult to thread a needle with a short strand of cotton and help you sew the hair on top of the sock puppet so that it sits above the eyes.

12 Put your hand back in the sock puppet and get playing!

SHOEBOX DOLL'S HOUSE

YOU WILL NEED:

2 cardboard shoeboxes (with lids)

A pencil

A ruler

Scissors

A roll of sticky tape

Patterned wrapping paper

A glue stick

2 large pieces of felt

Use leftover shoeboxes to make this simple but sturdy house for your toys. Once you've finished your doll's house, use paints and stickers to decorate it. You can also make furniture from scraps of cardboard and small everyday objects.

METHOD:

1 Remove the lids from the cardboard boxes and put them to one side.

2 Turn 1 shoebox onto its side so that the long panel is facing upwards and the opening is nearest you. Use a pencil and ruler to draw a 4cm x 10cm rectangle towards the top right-hand side of the panel.

3 Ask an adult to help you cut out the rectangle. This will be the opening where the ladder joins the ground and first floors of the house.

4 Place the first shoebox neatly on top of the second so that the hole is facing down. Use a pencil to draw around the hole in the first box so that you have a matching rectangle on the second box.

5 Ask an adult to help you cut out the rectangle. Line up the shorter ends of the 2 rectangular cut-outs and stick them together with tape. This will be the ladder that joins the ground and first floors of the house.

6 Turn the second shoebox so that the long, uncut panel is facing you. Ask an adult to help cut a 4cm x 4cm square hole in the opposite corner from the ladder opening. This will be the way into the attic.

CRAFTY TIP:

If you want to make a bigger doll's house, ask your adult to help you use large cardboard boxes to scale up the design.

7 Take the square piece of cardboard and trace around it to make a window shape in the middle of each shorter panel on both of the cardboard boxes. Ask an adult to help you cut out the 4 windows.

8 Take the 5 square pieces of cardboard. Line them up and stick them together with tape. This will be the ladder that joins the first floor to the attic.

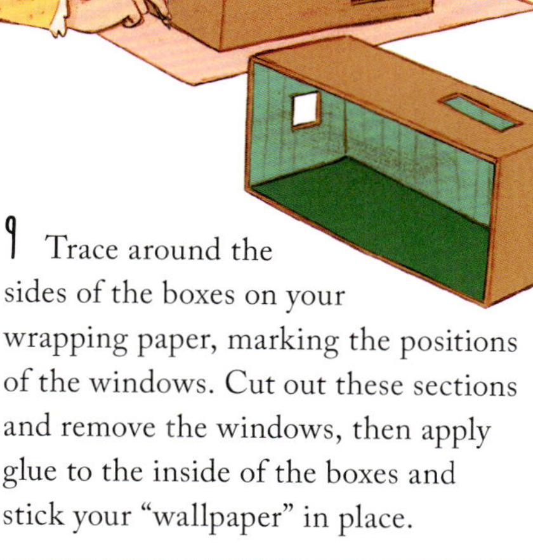

9 Trace around the sides of the boxes on your wrapping paper, marking the positions of the windows. Cut out these sections and remove the windows, then apply glue to the inside of the boxes and stick your "wallpaper" in place.

10 Trace around the bottoms of the boxes on pieces of felt, marking the ladder opening in one. Cut the sheets to size and remove the ladder opening. Apply glue to the floors of each box, then stick your "carpets" in place.

11 Apply glue to the top of the lower cardboard box and the bottom of the top cardboard box. Make sure the ladder openings align, then stick the boxes together.

12 To make the attic, ask an adult to flatten both of the cardboard lids and cut away the rims around the edges.

13 Cut 1 of the cardboard lids in half (lengthwise) so that you have 2 long strips. Use tape to attach the short edge of 1 strip to the top of the house. Repeat with the other strip on the opposite side, then lean them together and tape in place.

14 Cut the remaining cardboard lid into a series of panels that fit neatly across the back of the attic. Stick them in place with tape to make a slatted wall.

15 Trim the leftover pieces of card and stick them onto your ladder with a little glue, to make rungs. Lean your ladders in place (or use tape to attach them to the openings in the ceilings).

FILL YOUR HOUSE!

Cardboard stools: Ask an adult to help you cut an empty toilet roll into 3 rings. Cover with a circle of felt and stick in place to make a soft stool.

Cotton-reel table: Ask an adult if they have a finished reel of thread. Stick a small circle of cardboard on top to make a tiny table.

Lollipop frames: Stick 4 lollipop sticks together to make a square frame, then glue a picture or photo under the frame and hang it up.

Toilet-roll Maracas

These easy-to-make maracas are perfect for when you're feeling musical. Filled with rice, they make a satisfying sound when shaken.

You will need:

3 cardboard toilet rolls

Scissors

A pencil

1 piece of cardboard (about 12cm x 12cm)

A roll of sticky tape

2 handfuls of rice (uncooked)

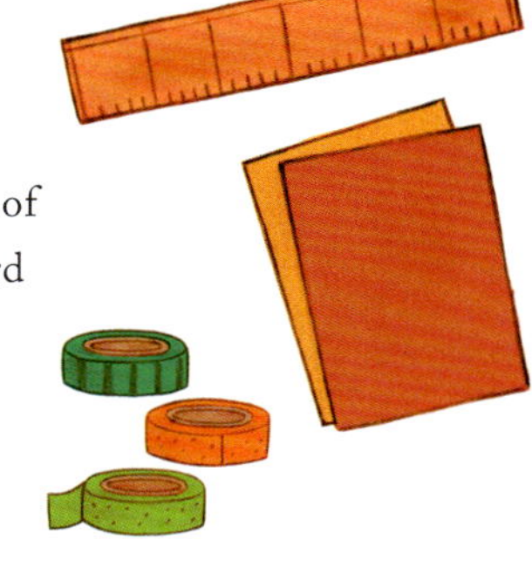

A ruler

2 A4 sheets of coloured card

Rolls of colourful paper tape

Method:

1 Start by making the handle for your maracas. Take 1 toilet roll tube and cut it in half (lengthwise).

2 Roll each half, as tightly as you can, into a tube. Use lots of tape to hold the tubes in place.

3 Take another toilet roll. Stand it on your piece of cardboard and draw around it. Cut out the circle.

4 Put the circle back onto the cardboard, draw around it and cut out another circle.

5 Repeat step 4 until you have 4 discs.

6 Ask an adult to wiggle the pointed end of a pencil through the middle of 2 of the cardboard discs, then remove the pencil and insert 1 tube through each hole. You can make the holes a little bigger if your tubes won't fit.

7 Wiggle the tubes further into the discs, leaving enough of the rolled tubes to use as handles, then stick the discs in place with tape.

8 Attach each "handle disc" to the bottom of a toilet roll tube with lots of tape, making sure they are securely fastened.

9 Fill each shaker with a handful of rice, then add the remaining cardboard discs on top of each maraca and fasten with lots of tape.

10 Place 1 of the filled maracas on an A4 sheet of card. Use a ruler and pencil to mark where the top and bottom of the toilet roll sit, then draw 2 lines along the length of the card.

11 Cut along the lines. Wrap the card around the maraca, sticking the ends of the card together with tape.

12 Repeat steps 10–11 so that you have 2 card-wrapped maracas.

13 Wrap strips of paper tape around the maracas, including the handles, alternating colours to make a stripy pattern.

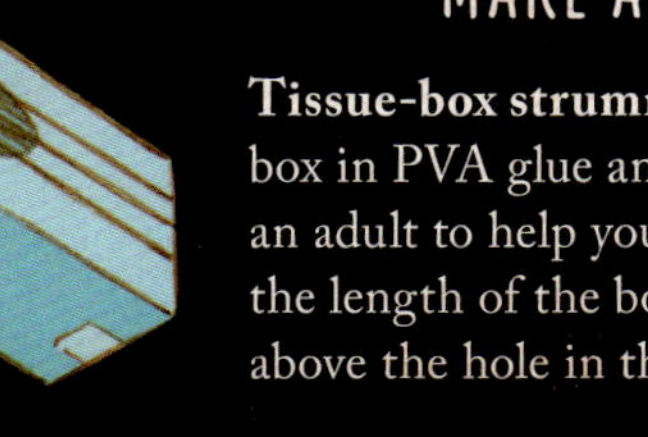

MAKE AN ORCHESTRA!

Tissue-box strummer: Cover an empty tissue box in PVA glue and pretty tissue paper. Ask an adult to help you stretch 3 rubber bands over the length of the box so that the "strings" sit above the hole in the tissue box.

Water-glass harmonies: Fill 3 water glasses with different amounts of water. Wet your finger, then run it smoothly around the rim of each glass. Can you hear the different sounds the glasses make?

Paper-straw pipes: Take 6 paper straws and cut off the ends, gradually snipping off more until you have cascading heights. Stick the row of straws together, then blow across the top!

Seam-Stitched Teddy Bear

You will need:

1 A4 sheet of paper

A pencil

A roll of sticky tape

Scissors

2 pieces of pretty fabric (each 20cm x 20cm)

A large, wide-eyed needle

6 sewing pins

A reel of cotton thread

Leftover scraps of fabric and wool

A fabric pen

Teddy bears are one of the best-loved toys ever! They're soft and cuddly. This project involves sewing with a needle, which takes time and practice. Don't worry if your sewing isn't neat, the stitches will be hidden on the inside of the bear.

Method:

1 Fold the paper in half, then use your pencil to draw an outline of half a teddy bear across the middle of the paper. You are looking for the teddy to be about 8cm wide and 20cm high.

2 Keep the paper folded, then cut around the pencil line. Open the paper back out so that you are left with a symmetrical template of a teddy bear!

3 Place the template on 1 piece of fabric, then stick in place using tape. Use your scissors to cut around the edge of the template, snipping the tape away as you go.

4 Repeat step 3 with the second piece of fabric so that you are left with 2 fabric bear shapes.

5 Put the 2 pieces of fabric together. If you are using fabric with a design on one side only, make sure the plain side is facing out on both pieces.

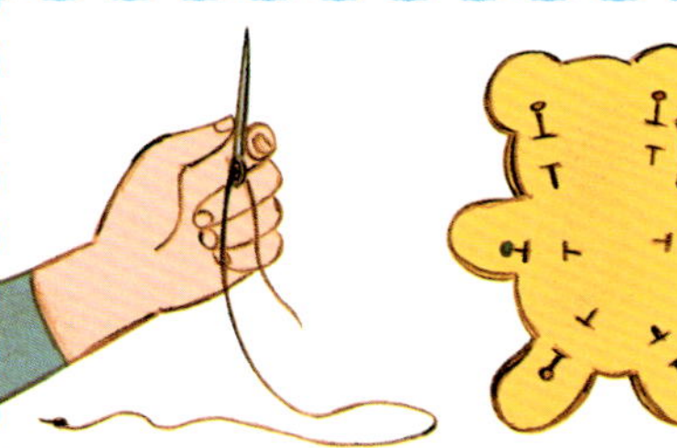

6 Ask an adult to help you thread the needle and tie a knot in the end of the thread. Then pin the 2 pieces of fabric together with sewing pins.

Crafty tip:

Turn to page 9 to see a step-by-step guide to sewing a running stitch.

7 Carefully poke the needle through both layers of fabric at the foot of the teddy bear (about 0.5cm from the edge). Pull the needle and thread through the fabric until the knot holds.

8 Ask an adult to help you do a simple running stitch around the edge (carefully removing any pins as you go). Your stitches should be about 0.5cm long and sit about 0.5cm from the edge of the fabric.

9 When you are nearly finished, stop sewing and leave a gap that is about 5cm wide. This is where the teddy bear stuffing will go in!

10 Tie off the stitch by threading your needle through the last stitch in the row. Bring the thread up, then tie it into a little knot. Cut the remaining thread away with scissors.

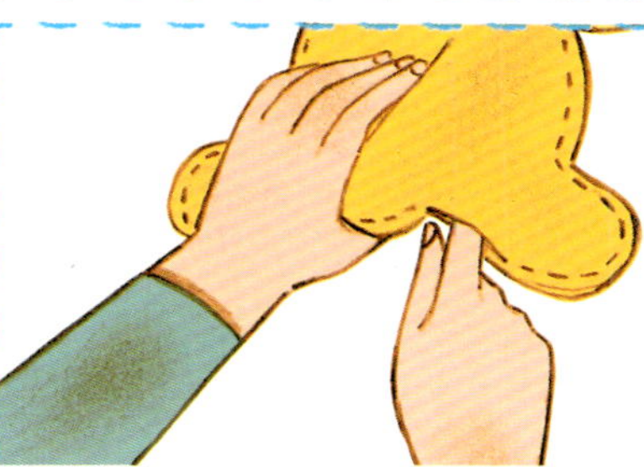

11 Wiggle your finger into the gap and gently pull the fabric from the inside of the bear so that the patterned fabric is on the outside.

12 Take time to neaten up the fabric so that it looks like a bear again.

13 Stuff the scraps of fabric and wool into the 5cm gap. Use your fingers to push the material to the edges of the bear to make sure all areas are stuffed.

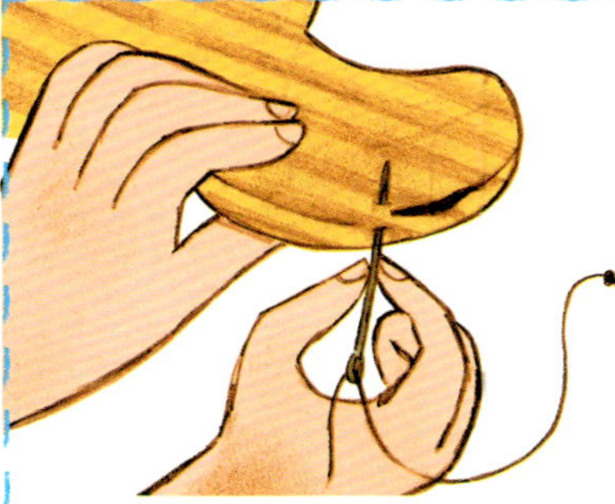

14 Do a few final stitches to close the gap on the bear (try and make them as neat as you can). Repeat step 10 to tie off the stitch.

15 Use your fabric pen to draw on eyes, a nose and a smile. You can even add decorations!

Accessorize your teddy:

Braided scarf: Braid together scraps of leftover fabric to make a simple scarf to tie around your teddy's neck.

Bedeck with buttons: Ask an adult to help you sew 3 buttons onto your bear's chest to make it look like they are wearing a waistcoat.

A downloadable teddy bear pattern can be found here: ***https://r.walker.co.uk/repairbear***

PAPIER-MÂCHÉ TIGER MASK

YOU WILL NEED:

A balloon

An old newspaper (or sheets of used paper)

PVA glue

A little tap water

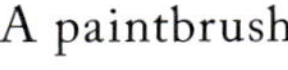

A paintbrush

Scissors

A piece of orange card (at least 6cm x 6cm)

A roll of sticky tape

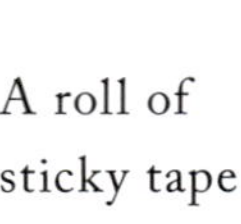

A pencil

Orange, white, pink and black poster paints

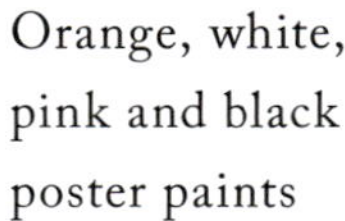

A 20cm piece of elastic thread

CRAFTY TIP:

Follow steps 1-7 to make a basic mask, then decorate it however you like. You could even make an alien mask to go with your rocket!

In this activity, we build papier mâché around a balloon using newspaper and glue to create a strong, light mask. We'll be painting the mask with a tiger face, but you can try out lots of different ideas, too.

METHOD:

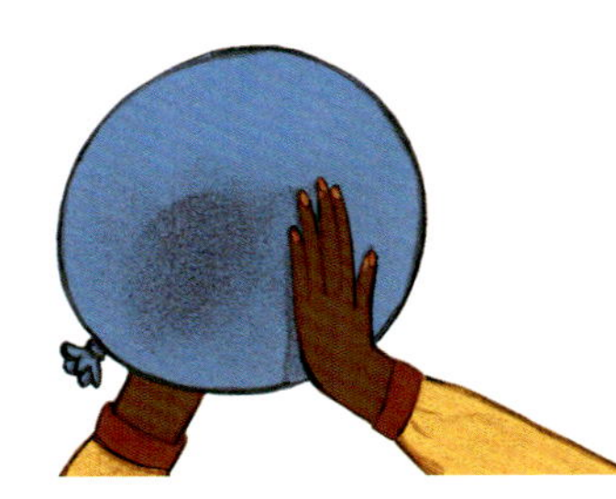

1 Ask an adult to help you blow up a balloon until it is a little bigger than the size of your head, then tie off the end.

2 Tear up the newspaper into strips and lay them on a wipe-clean surface.

3 Pour a big blob of PVA glue into a little bowl, then add twice the amount of water to the bowl. Stir the mixture together with your paintbrush.

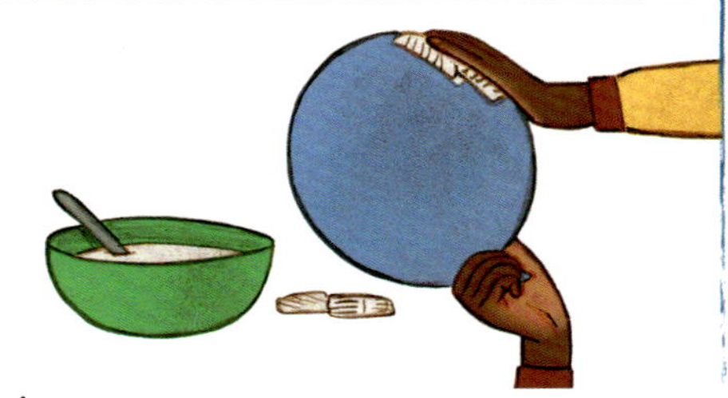

4 Dip the strips of newspaper into the glue mixture and lay them onto 1 half of the balloon, smoothing them down as you go.

5 Keep applying gluey paper to the balloon until 1 half is covered. You may need to make more gluey-water mixture as you work.

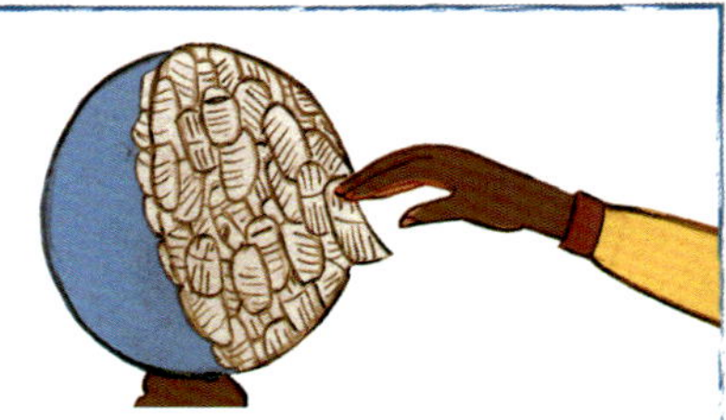

6 Once you have finished 1 layer, add another layer of gluey paper to your mask, and another, until you have about 6 layers of papier mâché. Leave to dry until the paper has gone stiff and shiny.

7 Ask an adult to help you pop the balloon with scissors, then gently pull the mask away from the balloon. Use your scissors to neaten up the edges of the mask.

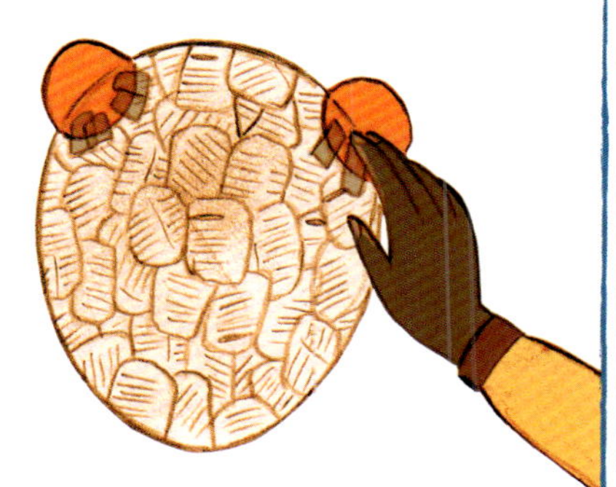

8 Cut 2 circles (measuring 3cm across) out of the orange card. Use a little tape to stick the circles to the top of the mask to make the ears.

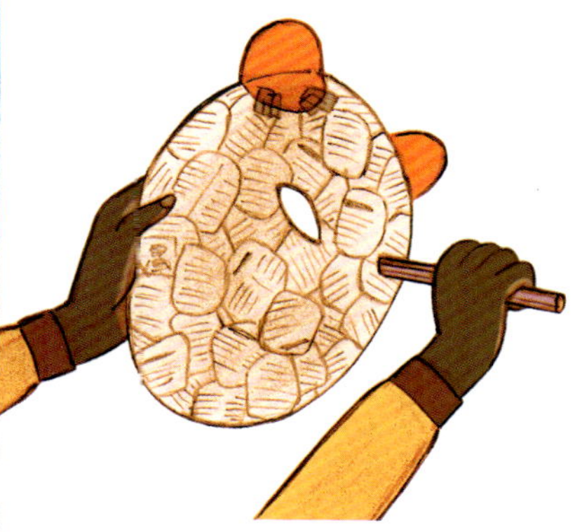

9 Ask an adult to wiggle the pointed end of a pencil into the mask to make 2 eye holes as well as 2 little holes, 1 on each side of the mask.

10 Paint your mask orange, then leave to dry. When the paint has set, use your white paint to add details around the outside of the mask and a white circle just below the centre of the face.

11 Leave the white paint to dry, then paint a nose onto the white circle with your pink paint. Use your black paint to add a mouth and whiskers in the white circle, then paint black stripes all around the mask.

12 Once the mask has dried, ask an adult to help you measure the width of the elastic you'll need to attach the mask around your head. Thread the elastic through the little holes on each side of the mask, then secure the elastic with knots. Slip the mask over your head and get playing!

ADD MORE TO YOUR MASK:

Cardboard add-ons: Cut out horns, ears or a crown shape and attach them to your mask with a little PVA glue.

Feathered friend: Stick colourful feathers onto your mask to make a bird mask. You could even add a cardboard beak.

YOU WILL NEED:

- 1 large plastic bottle (empty, clean and dry)
- Scissors
- 1 A4 sheet of card
- A roll of sticky tape
- An old newspaper
- PVA glue
- A little tap water
- A paintbrush
- Red, white and grey poster paints

PAPIER-MÂCHÉ ROCKET

Keep your papier-mâché skills fired up with this out-of-this-world activity where we re-use an old plastic bottle to make an amazing rocket!

CRAFTY TIP:

Once you've finished playing with your rocket, ask an adult to thread fairy lights through it and hang it in your bedroom as a rocket light.

METHOD:

1 Ask an adult to help you cut around the bottom of the bottle, removing 2–3cm from the base. Remove the bottle top and store it in your craft box.

2 Draw a "fin" shape measuring 10cm high and 4cm wide on the card. Cut it out, then repeat this so that you have 2 identical wings.

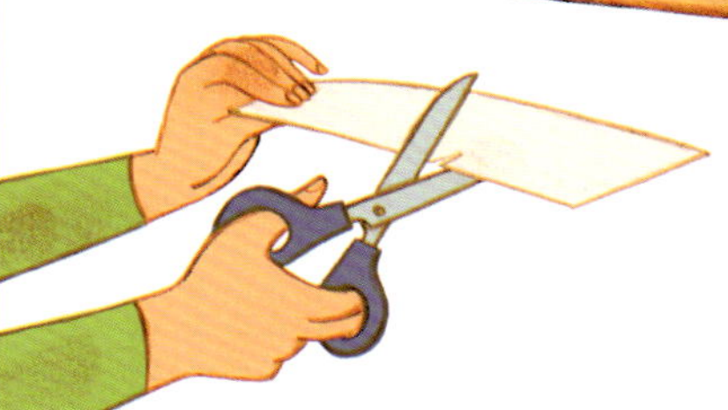

3 Fold the long straight edge of each wing in by 1cm, then make a snip in the middle as far as the fold line to create 2 flaps. Bend 1 flap forwards and 1 flap backwards.

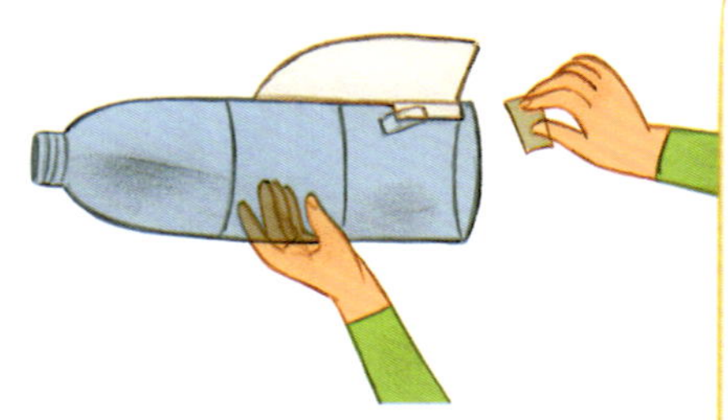

4 Place 1 wing on each side of the bottle and stick the little flaps in place with some tape.

5 Tear the newspaper into strips. Pour a big blob of PVA glue into a bowl, then add twice as much water. Stir the mixture together with your paintbrush.

6 Dip the strips of paper in the glue mixture and lay them all over the rocket shape (including the wings), smoothing them down. Press the newspaper up to the bottle-top opening.

7 Once you have 1 layer that covers the entire surface, keep adding more layers until you have about 6 layers of papier mâché. Leave to dry until the paper has gone stiff and shiny.

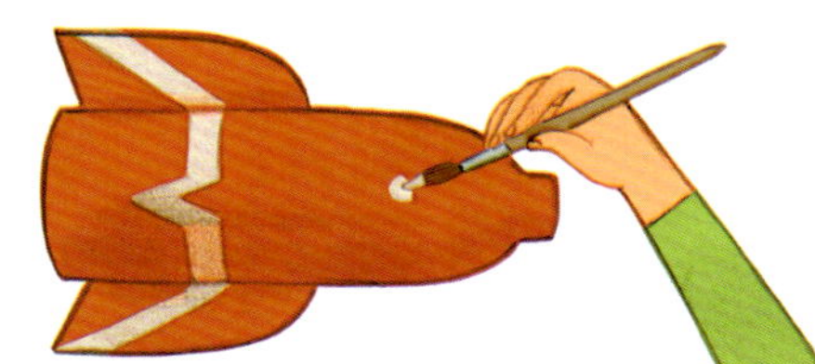

8 Paint the rocket all over with red poster paint. Once the paint has dried, use your white and grey paints to add windows to the middle of the rocket and details to the wings.

9 Once the paint has dried, paint on a thin layer of PVA glue, to give your rocket a super-shiny finish.

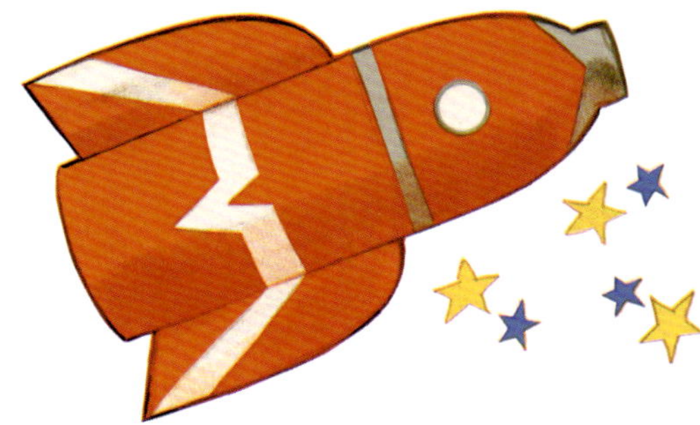

PERFECT PRESENTS

Pop-up Present Cards

You will need:

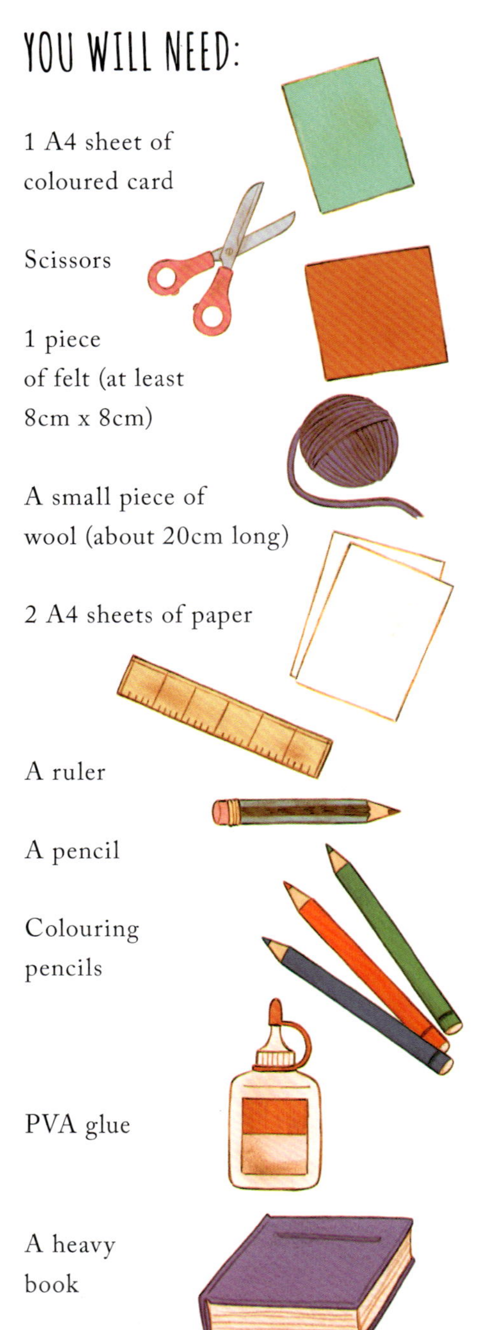

1 A4 sheet of coloured card

Scissors

1 piece of felt (at least 8cm x 8cm)

A small piece of wool (about 20cm long)

2 A4 sheets of paper

A ruler

A pencil

Colouring pencils

PVA glue

A heavy book

These fun and interactive cards are perfect to give with a handmade gift. Surprise your friends and family as they reveal your pop-up design when they open the card.

Method:

1 Fold the sheet of card in half. Unfold and cut down the fold line so that you have 2 equal pieces.

2 Fold both pieces of card in half, pressing down along the fold line with your finger to make sure that the fold is nice and neat.

3 Start by decorating the front of each card. Cut a 4cm x 4cm square of felt. Tie a little piece of wool into a bow, stick it onto the felt, then stick the square onto the card.

4 Repeat steps 1–2 with 1 sheet of paper so that you are left with 2 pieces of folded paper.

5 Take 1 of the folded pieces of paper and make 4 parallel snips (measuring 4cm long) from the fold line out. The folded paper should look like an "E" shape.

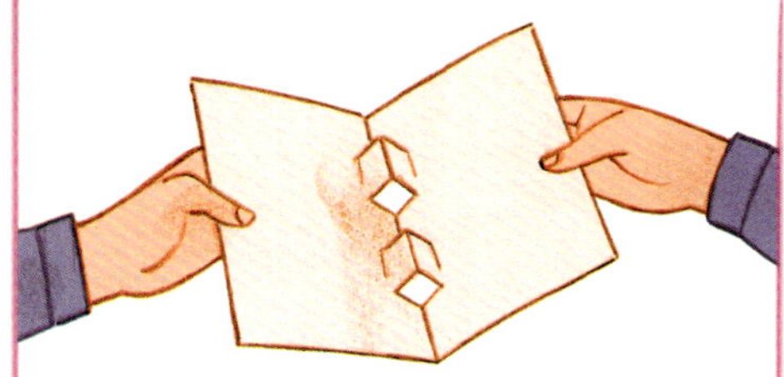

6 Open up the paper and use your fingers to carefully pull the 2 tabs of paper inwards.

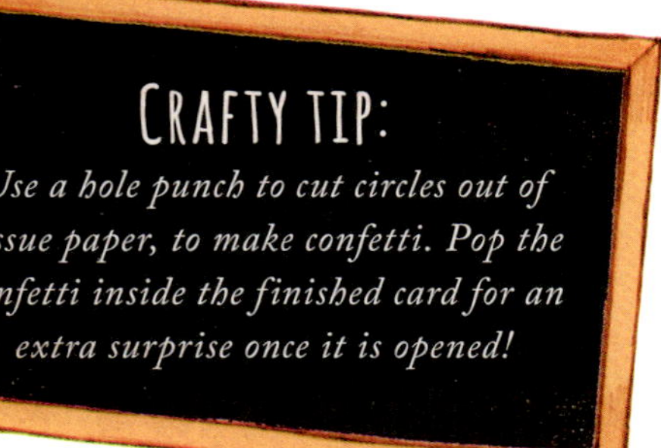

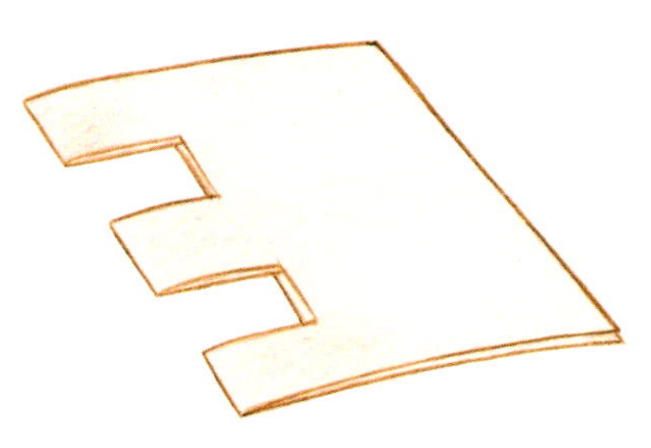

7 Close the paper so that the tabs fold in on themselves. When you open the paper up again, the tabs should have a fold down the middle and stick out from the paper. Repeat steps 5–7 with your second piece of folded paper.

8 Open the folded cards and lay them flat on a surface. Dab PVA glue around the edges.

9 Line each piece of card with a tabbed piece of paper and press down until secured to the card.

10 Use your pencil to draw little flowers, hearts or animals on the remaining sheet of paper. Make sure that they are small enough to fit on the tabs inside the card.

11 Carefully cut around your drawings and gently stick them onto the tabs, being careful not to glue over the centre folds. You can also stick drawings around the tabs.

12 Leave your cards open as they dry. Once the glue has set, close your cards and use a heavy book to weigh them down. Leave for 10 minutes, then open up your cards and see them pop!

MAKE A SIMPLE ENVELOPE!

1. Use a ruler and pencil to measure 4cm in from the short edge of an A4 sheet of paper and make a pencil mark.
2. Bring the other short edge of the paper up and over to the pencil mark, then smooth it down so that you have a folded sheet of paper with a flap.
3. Unfold the paper, then apply glue along the edges of the 2 sides.
4. Fold the paper together and hold in place.
5. Fold the flap of the paper over, pressing down hard to make sure the fold line works.
6. Once you have filled your envelope, stick the flap in place with tape.

Marbled-paper writing set

You will need:

A large tray (at least 3cm deep)

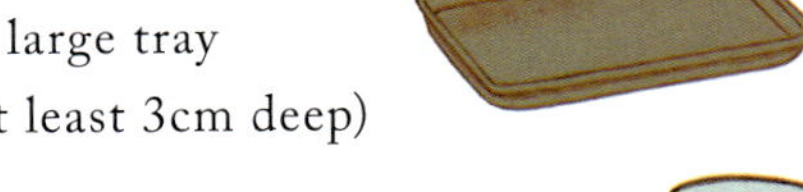

A glass of tap water

A tablespoon

2 tablespoons of vegetable oil

Blue and green food colouring (liquid)

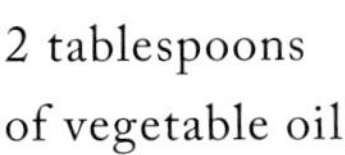

2 paper bowls

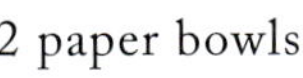

7 sheets of A4 paper

Scissors

A reel of twine or a ball of wool

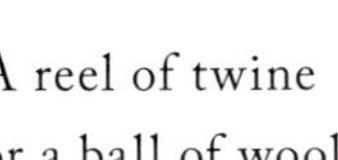

A hole punch

A pen

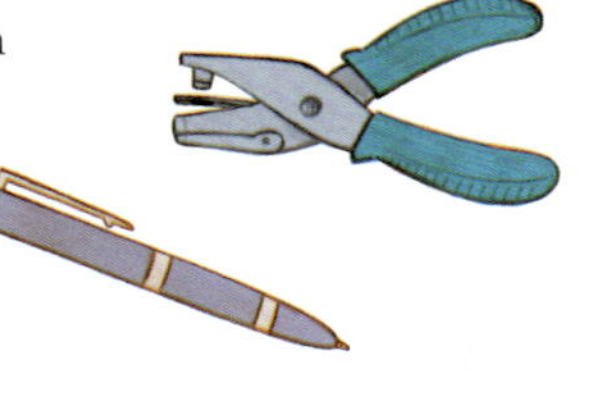

Crafty tip:

Marbling can be messy and the ink can stain. Make sure you do your marbling over a wipe-clean surface.

It is so lovely to receive a letter in the post. These pretty paper sheets, tied together with twine, make a perfect gift for anyone who likes to write letters. Use your leftover marbled paper to make gift tags or keep them for another craft project.

Method:

1 Fill your tray with tap water, until it is about 2cm deep.

2 Add 1 tablespoon of oil to a paper bowl, then start to add a few drops of blue food colouring. Stir together until the colour starts to mix into the oil.

3 Add 1 tablespoon of oil and a few drops of green food colouring to the second paper bowl and mix together.

4 Use your tablespoon to add drops of blue and green oil to the tray, then swirl them around a little until you can see a pattern.

5 Hold 1 sheet of paper over the tray, then lower it in until the paper touches the surface.

6 Gently swirl the paper around the tray, then lift it out, turn it over and leave it to dry on a wipe-clean surface.

7 Repeat steps 5–6, until all 7 sheets of paper have a pretty, marbled pattern.

8 Leave your paper to dry on a wipe-clean surface (this may take 3 hours).

9 Once the paper is completely dry, carefully fold 6 of the sheets in half (widthwise).

10 Open the 6 sheets of paper up again, then cut down the fold line, until you have 12 pieces of paper.

11 Stack the pages on top of each other (marbled side facing up). Cut about 50cm of twine, hold it up and fold it in half.

12 Loop the twine under the stack of paper. Bring the ends back over the paper, fastening the twine in place with a knot.

13 Take your remaining sheet of paper and cut out a heart shape (about 4cm x 4cm). This will be your gift tag. Put any leftover marbled paper in your craft box.

14 Use a hole punch to make a little hole in the gift tag. Add a name or message to the front, then thread the tag onto the twine.

MAKE USE OF YOUR MARBLING!

Place settings: Add some fun to a family meal by making little place holders with each of your family's names on. Simply fold a little piece of marbled paper in half and write a name in your neatest handwriting on the front.

Gift tags: Use a hole punch to make a little hole in any leftover bits of marbled paper. Thread a ribbon through to make more gift tags.

Découpage decorations: Cut out scraps of marbled paper into beautiful shapes like hearts, stars or diamonds and use them for a découpage craft (see page 36).

WOVEN SWEETIE BOWLS

YOU WILL NEED:

1 paper bowl

Scissors

Balls of red, orange and green wool

A wide-eyed needle

A small paintbrush

Red, orange and green poster paints (or 3 of your favourite colours)

1 sheet of tissue paper

A 20cm length of ribbon

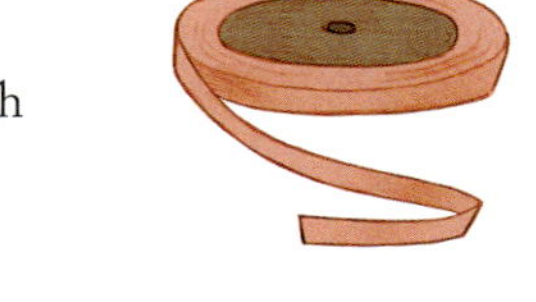

Paper bowls are often used for party food, but we're going to transform one into a beautiful woven bowl. To make it more fun, you can choose a selection of wrapped sweets to fill your bowl. Match your wool colours to your sweets so that the bowl looks even sweeter.

METHOD:

1 Ask an adult to help snip the bowl from the rim down to the base. Cut 7 snips all the way around, making sure they are evenly spaced.

2 Spool out a little red wool into your hand, then wiggle the end of the wool through the first snip, pushing it down until it touches the base.

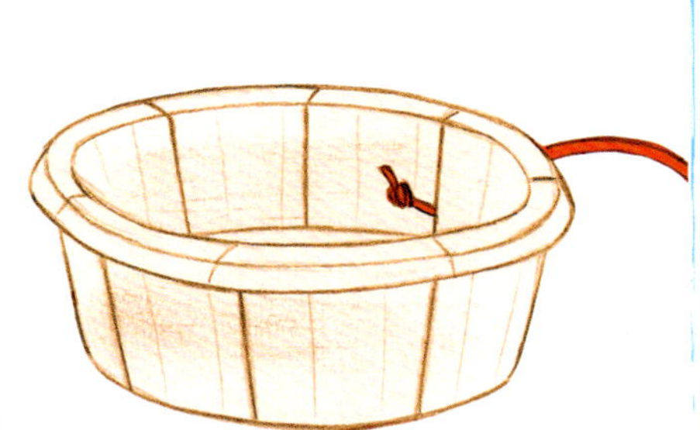

3 Fasten the wool in place by tying a knot in the end inside the bowl. Don't worry, you won't be able to see the knot once you start weaving.

4 Guide the wool through the 7 snips in the bowl, making sure that you alternate weaving over and under each panel and keep the wool as taut as possible as you weave.

CRAFTY TIP:

This project is the perfect thing for using up any little scraps of wool, as you can alternate the choice of wool as you weave.

5 Keep weaving until you have a few rows of the red wool, then snip the end off the red wool and tie on a piece of orange wool, fastening them together with a little knot.

6 Keep weaving until you have a few rows of orange wool, then repeat step 5 with your green wool.

7 Keep alternating different colours of wool until you reach the top of the bowl, just under the paper rim.

8 Ask your adult to help you thread the end of the wool through your needle, then wiggle the needle back under a few lines of the woven wool. Snip away any excess wool.

9 Add colour to the rim and base using your paints. You could even create a fun pattern.

10 Leave your little bowl to dry. Once it is ready, fill it with sweets, wrap it in a sheet of tissue paper, tie with a ribbon and give it to a friend as a gift.

CRAFTY TIP:

Fill your gift bowl with sweet fruit or a friend's favourite snacks.

TAWNY OWL PINCUSHION

YOU WILL NEED:

- 1 sheet of A4 paper
- A pencil
- A ruler
- Scissors
- 1 A4 sheet of light brown felt
- A roll of sticky tape
- A wide-eyed needle
- A reel of cotton thread
- Leftover scraps of fabric and wool
- PVA glue
- A fabric pen
- 12 sewing pins

CRAFTY TIP:

Turn to page 9 to find out how to thread your needle and stitch fabric.

This little felt pincushion is the perfect present for any keen crafter and will help you refine your sewing skills as you make it. The instructions below are for crafting an owl, but the design can be adapted to become either a fox, pig or even a panda!

METHOD:

1 Ask an adult to help you draw a cross-shaped template on your paper made up of 5cm x 5cm squares. The template should be 4 squares high and 3 squares wide.

2 Cut out the paper template and place it on your sheet of felt. Use little pieces of tape to hold the template in place.

3 Ask your adult to help you cut around the template, snipping away the tape as you go, until you are left with a piece of felt that is a cross shape.

4 Fold the short flap at the top of the cross down, then fold 1 side panel in, until the 2 panels touch.

5 Pinch the 2 panels together with your fingers, then ask your adult to carefully wiggle the needle through both pieces of felt so that the tops of the panels are held together in place.

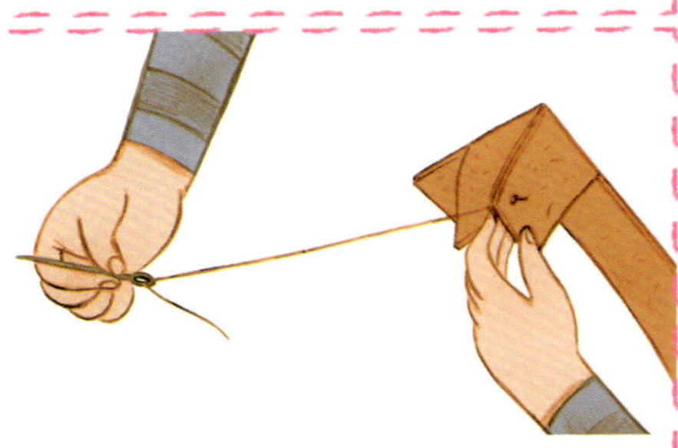

6 With help from your adult, thread the needle (and knot the end of the thread), then pull the thread through the felt until it holds in place.

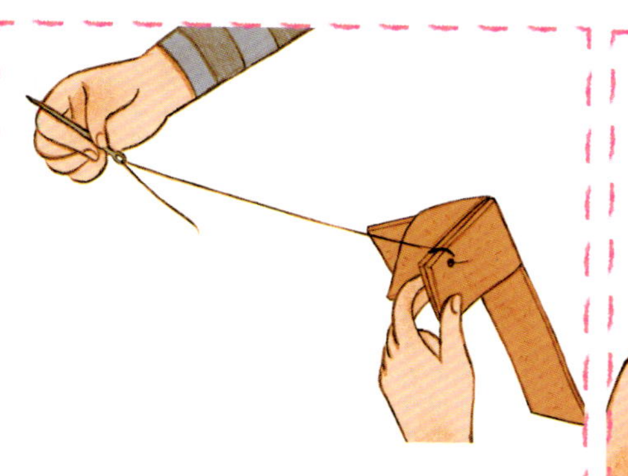

7 Stitch all the way up the panels, pinching the felt together and weaving your thread through both pieces so that the stitches pull the edges of the panels neatly together.

8 When you get to the corner, weave the needle back through the last 2 stitches in the row, then wiggle the needle back into the felt. Use your scissors to trim away the excess thread.

9 Fold the other side panel in and repeat steps 5–8 to sew it in place.

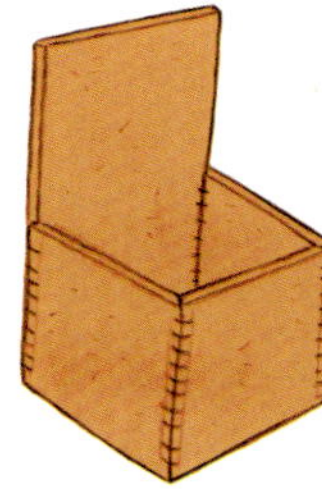

10 Fold the longest panel up, then sew half of the long panel in place so that you have a box shape with 1 remaining flap of felt not yet sewn down.

11 Stuff the open box with the scraps of fabric and wool, making sure that the material is packed in nice and snug.

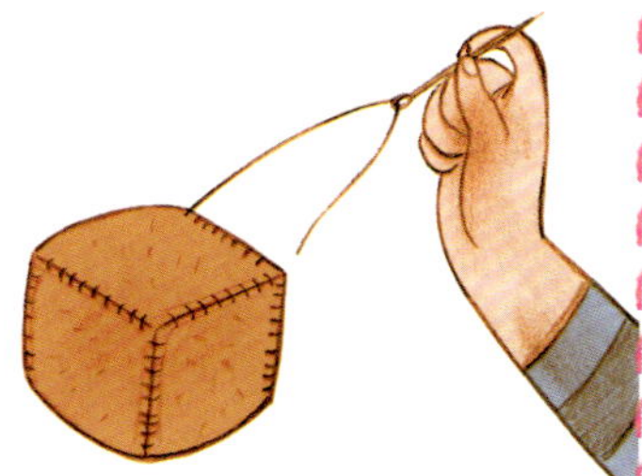

12 Once the felt box is full, cover it with the final panel. Ask your adult to help you sew the remaining seams in place to seal the box.

13 Turn the cube over so that the stitches on the last panel are on the bottom. Cut out wings, feet and a tail from the scraps of leftover felt, then sew or stick them onto the cube.

14 Draw on eyes and a little beak using a fabric pen. Once your owl is complete, carefully push the sewing pins into the top of the cube to make a pincushion!

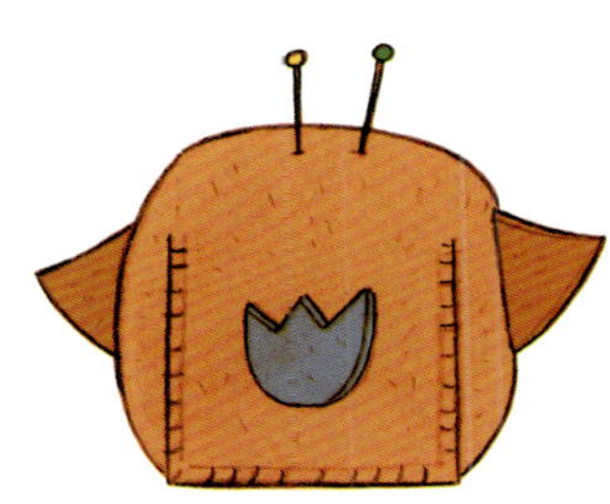

MAKE A PINCUSHION WOODLAND!

Fox: Use a fabric pen to draw little paws, pointy ears and a nose on an orange pincushion to make a fox. Cut any leftover white and orange felt out to make a tail, then stick it onto the pincushion.

Pig: Make little pink ears, a round nose and a curly tail from pink felt and stick them onto a light pink pincushion.

Panda: Cut out felt ears and paws from black felt and stick them onto a white felt pincushion to make a cute panda.

Keepsake Heart Keyring

You will need:

An old keyring

A small piece of leather (or denim or felt, at least 9cm x 9cm)

A scrap of paper

Scissors

A felt-tip pen

A hole punch

A glue gun

A heavy book

A sheet of baking paper

A 20cm length of ribbon

For this activity, you can use a small piece of leather to make a stunning keepsake. Ask a family member for an old handbag or jacket that you could use. Don't worry if you can't find any leather; you can use denim or felt instead.

Method:

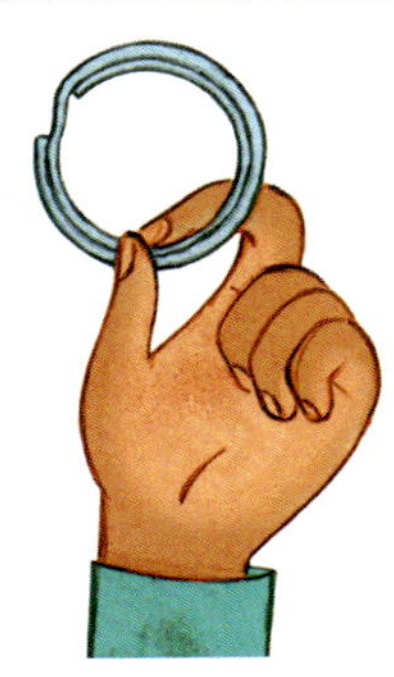

1 Ask an adult to help remove the old item from the keyring so you are left with just the metal loop.

2 Take your scrap of leather and turn it upside down so that the rougher side is facing you.

3 Use your felt-tip pen to draw a heart shape (about 4cm x 4cm) on your scrap piece of paper and cut it out.

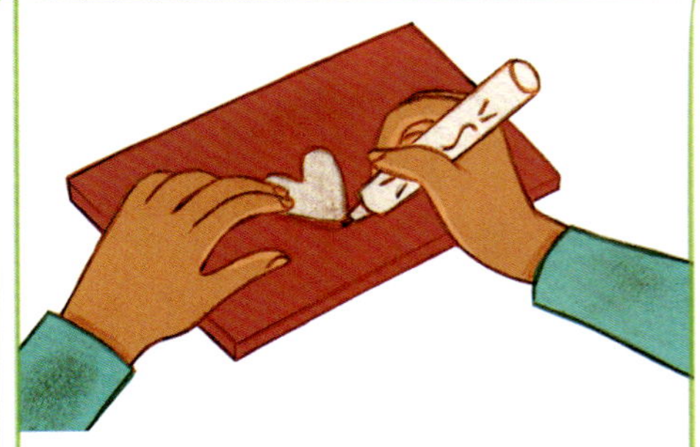

4 Place the heart shape on the piece of leather and draw around it twice.

5 Ask your adult to carefully cut around the outlines so that you have 2 identical leather heart shapes.

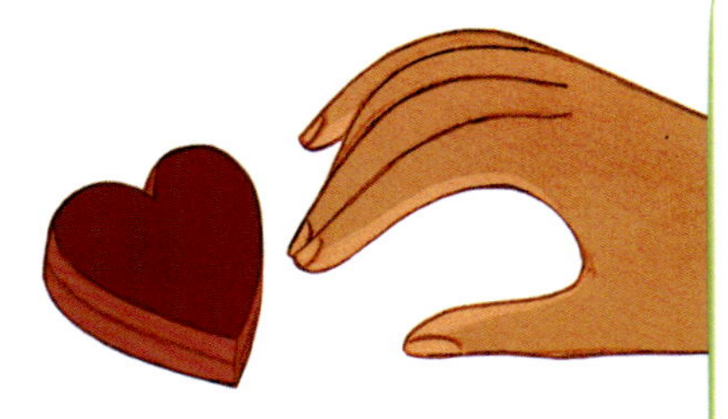

6 Put the hearts together with the rougher sides facing in and the smooth sides facing out. Make sure that the outlines are perfectly aligned.

Crafty Tip:

Leather can be quite a tough material so ask an adult to help you with the cutting and hole-punching steps in this activity.

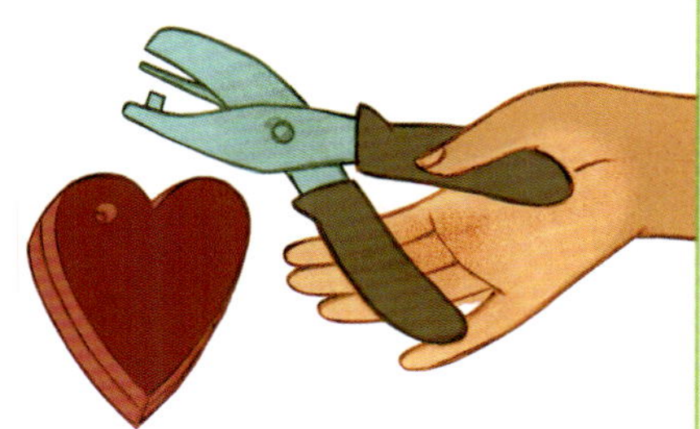

7 Ask your adult to punch a hole in the top left-hand corner, being careful not to punch the hole too close to the edge. If the punch doesn't go through both layers, punch each layer in turn – just make sure that the holes align!

8 Place the heart shapes back on a wipe-clean surface, then ask your adult to help you dab glue onto the rougher sides of the leather. Take care, glue guns can get very hot.

9 Stick the leather hearts together so that the holes align and you are left with a smooth-sided heart shape.

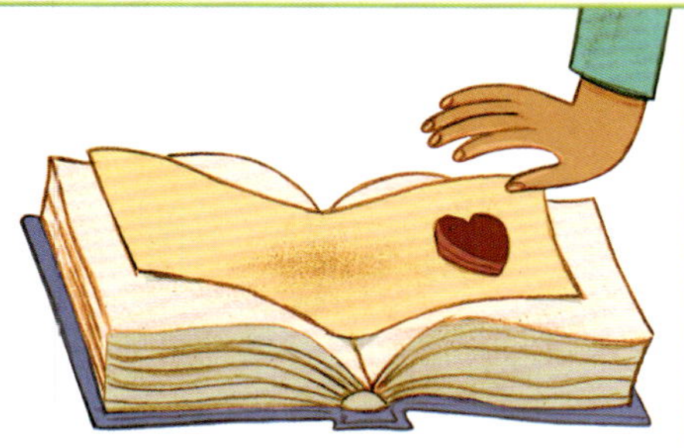

10 Open the heavy book, line with a little baking paper, then place the leather heart inside. Close the book and leave the leather to bond together.

11 Once the leather has completely stuck together, remove it from the book and thread the ribbon through the hole.

12 Thread the top ends of the ribbon through the keyring loop, then tie them together so that the leather heart is securely fastened to the keyring.

MORE KEYRING IDEAS!

Braided keyring: Turn to page 40 to find out how to braid, then attach your creation to an old metal keyring loop.

Pom-pom keyring: Turn to page 74 to find out how to make a pom-pom, then tie it to the end of your keyring.

Beaded keyring: Loop a little gardening wire around the end of a keyring, thread on lots of pretty beads, then tie the ends of the wire.

Upcycled keyring: Ask an adult to help you prise open an old, plastic photo keyring that has a picture inside it. Remove the picture and replace it with a little piece of paper with a saying, a dried flower or even a drawing.

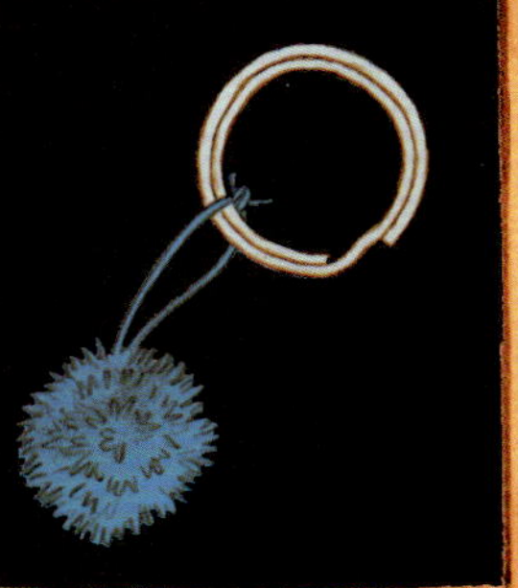

Star-print table runner

You will need:

1 old cotton tablecloth (or a long length of cotton fabric)

A ruler

A felt-tip pen

Scissors

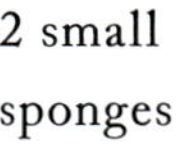

2 small sponges

Green and yellow poster paints (or 2 of your favourite colours)

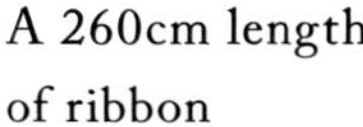

A 260cm length of ribbon

PVA glue

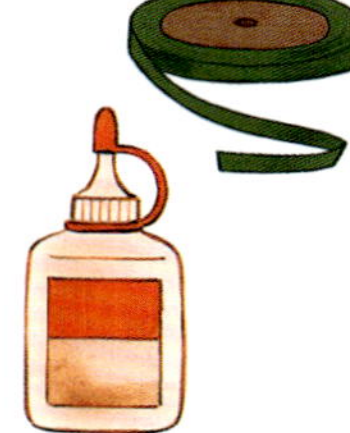

Printing with paint is so much fun. Ask an adult if they have an old cotton tablecloth, or a big length of material that they're happy for you to print. Then cut a sponge into a simple star shape (or any shape you like), dip it in some colourful paint and let your imagination soar!

Method:

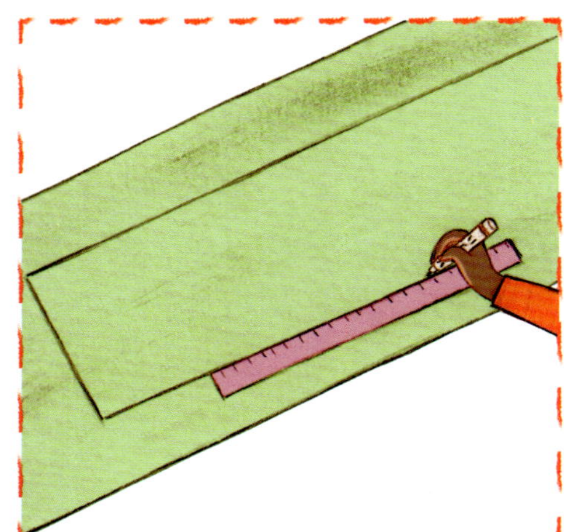

1 Ask an adult to help you measure a 100cm x 30cm rectangle from your unused tablecloth. Don't worry if your tablecloth is smaller than this – just cut it to whatever length you can (and keep it to about 30cm wide).

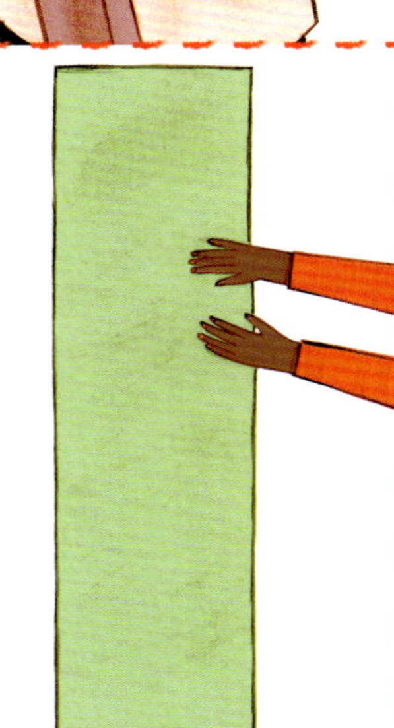

2 Lay the fabric out on a wipe-clean surface. Put any remaining scraps of fabric in your craft box for another craft project.

3 Take your sponges and draw a star shape on each with a felt-tip pen. Draw a big star on 1 sponge and a smaller star on the other sponge.

4 Ask your adult to help you cut around the star shapes until you have 2 3-D stars.

Crafty tip:

If you have one, you can use a metre ruler or a measuring tape to more easily measure long lengths of fabric.

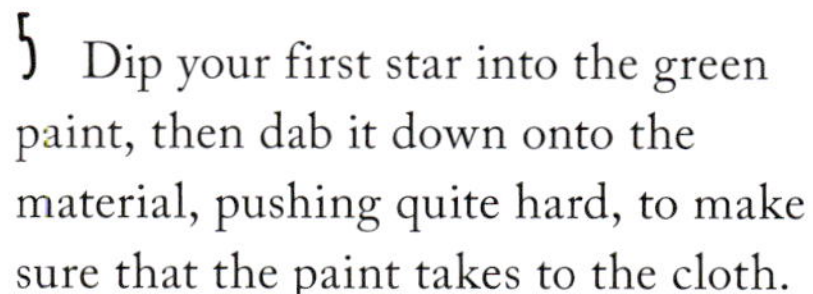

5 Dip your first star into the green paint, then dab it down onto the material, pushing quite hard, to make sure that the paint takes to the cloth.

6 Dip your other star into the yellow paint and dab it down, near to your first star print.

7 Print as many stars as you would like on the table runner. Once you are happy with the pattern, leave it to dry.

8 Take your ribbon and cut 2 lengths measuring 30cm (or measure the ribbon against the width of the table runner). Ask your adult to help you snip the lengths at the end.

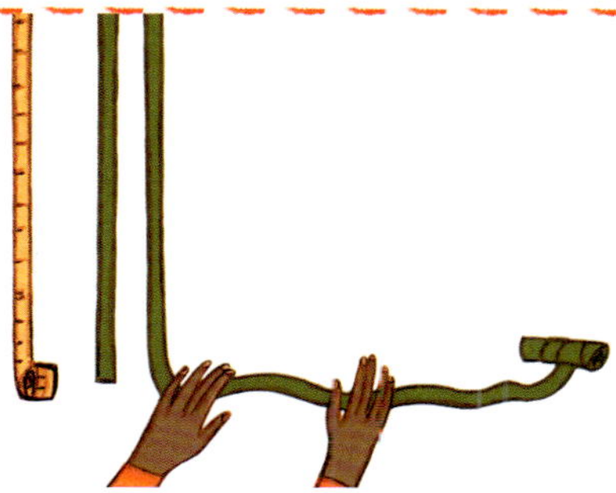

9 Measure 2 lengths of ribbon, each 1 metre long (or measure the ribbon against the length of the table runner), and snip the ends.

10 Apply glue to 1 of the lengths of ribbon, then press it in place along the edge of the runner, using your hands to smooth it down.

11 Stick the remaining pieces of ribbon in place, then leave to dry.

Sew-on clothes patches: Cut out star and heart shapes from scraps of printed material, then ask an adult to help you stitch them over any holes in your clothes.

Scented drawer bags: Place dried lavender in the centre of a small rectangular-shaped piece of material, gather the material together and tie it with a loop of wool. Place it in a drawer to keep your clothes smelling nice.

DÉCOUPAGE CRAFT BOX

YOU WILL NEED:

A cardboard shoebox (with lid)

Scissors

A roll of double-sided tape

A hole punch

A 30cm length of ribbon

PVA glue

A small paintbrush

2 sheets of tissue paper

A range of small images printed on paper (carefully cut out)

A pencil

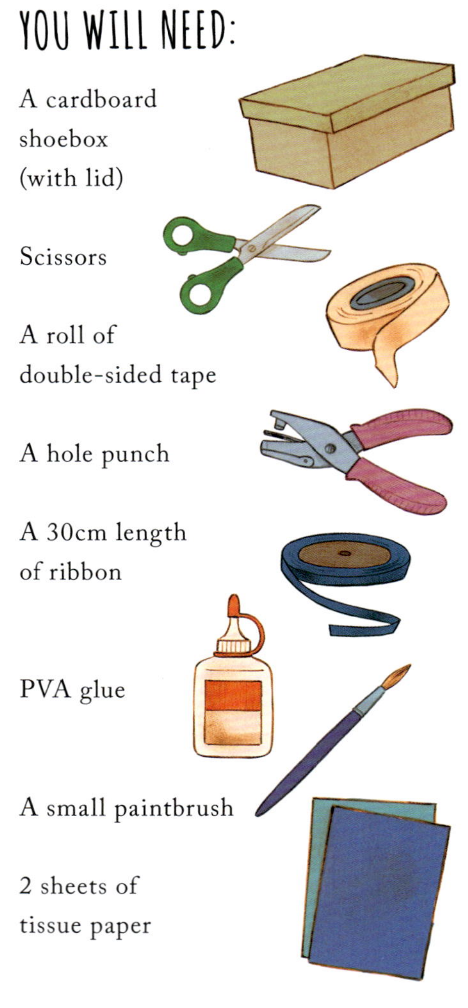

This activity gives you all the steps you need to make a decorative box for your crafting treasures. "Découpage" is the art of cutting out flat images and sticking them onto an object to give it a new lease of life. Look for pretty designs in magazines, wrapping paper or even old wallpaper, making sure you cut them out as neatly as you can.

METHOD:

1 Remove the cardboard lid from your cardboard box.

2 Ask an adult to help you cut up the corner edges of either side of the lid's long panel.

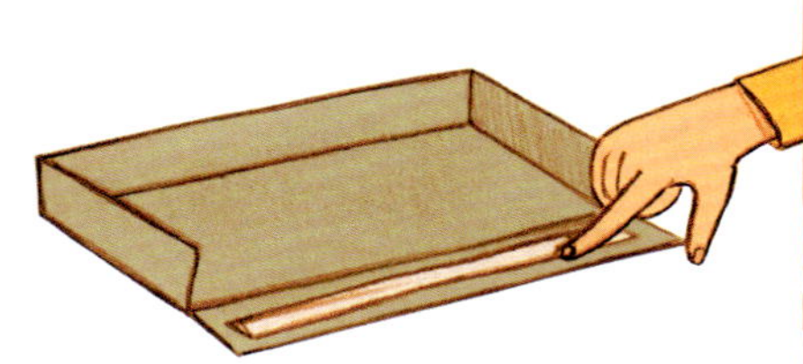

3 You should now have a long, loose flap on 1 side of the lid. Cut a length of double-sided tape and stick it to the inside of the flap.

4 Peel the backing off the tape, then stick the long flap onto the empty cardboard box to make a lid that is hinged to the box.

5 Use your hole punch to make a hole 5cm along the short side of the lid (nearest to the hinge) and 5cm along the short edge of the box (nearest to the hinge). Repeat on the other side.

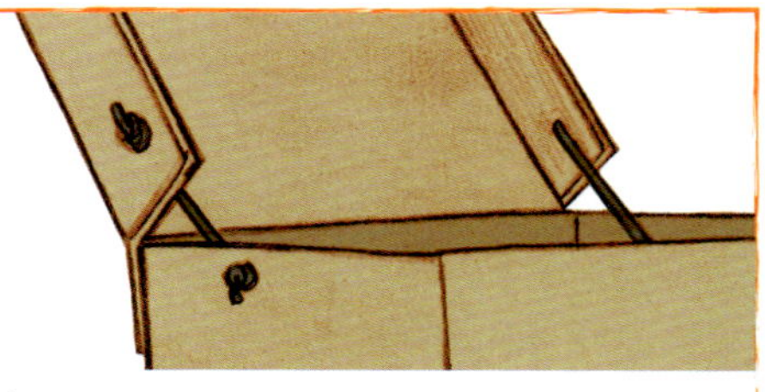

6 Ask your adult to help you cut the ribbon in half. Thread a ribbon through each hole in the box up to the hole in the lid and fasten in place with a knot either end.

7 Brush PVA glue over the top and sides of the lid and cover with strips of tissue paper (leave room between the lid and box so that the hinge still works).

8 Smooth the tissue paper strips down with your paintbrush, adding a little more glue to hold it all in place.

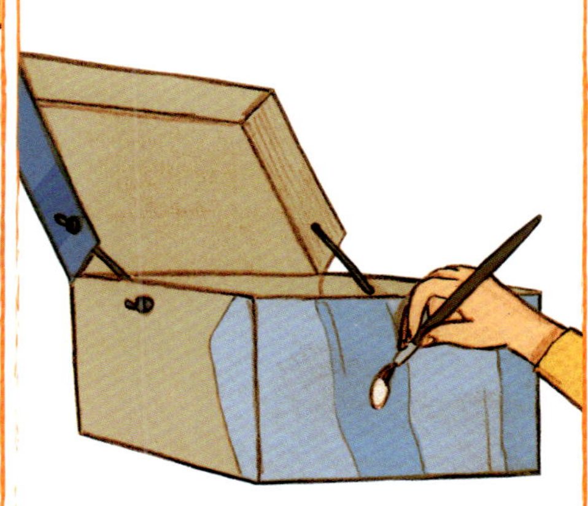

9 Leave the lid to dry, then repeat steps 7–8 with the cardboard box.

10 Once the lid and box have dried, arrange your images over the box until you are happy with how it looks.

11 Apply a fine layer of glue to the underside of each shape, then stick in place. Leave your box to dry (lid open).

12 Shut the lid and use your pencil to draw a lock shape on the front of the box so that the top of the lock sits on the lid and the bottom of the lock sits on the cardboard box.

13 When you open the craft box, it should look like the lock opens. Arrange your craft items in the box, then store the box until crafting inspiration strikes!

SALT-DOUGH NECKLACE

YOU WILL NEED:

150g plain flour

75g table salt

A mixing bowl

75ml tap water

A tablespoon

A baking tray

A sheet of baking paper

A wooden skewer

3 poster paints (choose your favourite colours)

A small paintbrush

Scissors

A 60cm length of wool

A large, wide-eyed needle

For this next craft activity, we use a simple salt dough mixture to make beautiful beads. Once the beads have dried, paint them whichever colour you like. You can even paint pretty patterns or letters on each bead. Thread the beads onto a strand of wool and, *voilà*, you have a perfect present.

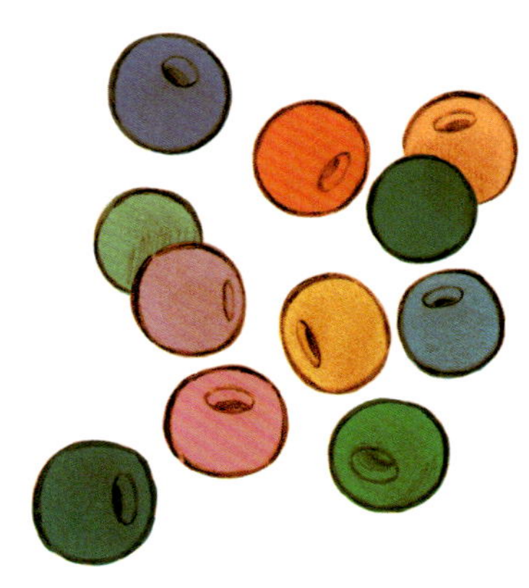

METHOD:

1 Mix the flour with the table salt in a mixing bowl. Add the water, 1 tablespoon at a time, stirring well.

2 When the dough starts to come together, add another couple of tablespoons of water, then use your hands to bring the mixture into a ball.

3 Line a large baking tray with baking paper and ask an adult to pre-heat the oven to 75°C (fan-assisted).

4 Roll the dough with your hands to make beads that are each about the size of a grape (roughly 2cm wide), then place the beads on the lined tray.

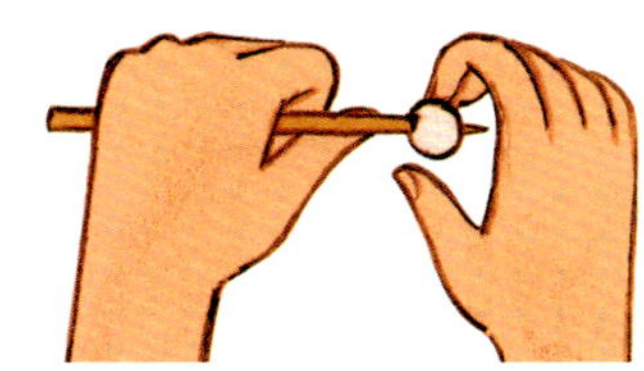

5 Ask an adult to help wiggle a wooden skewer through the middle of each bead. When you break through to the other side, gently wiggle the skewer out, then wiggle it back in and out again to make the hole look neat.

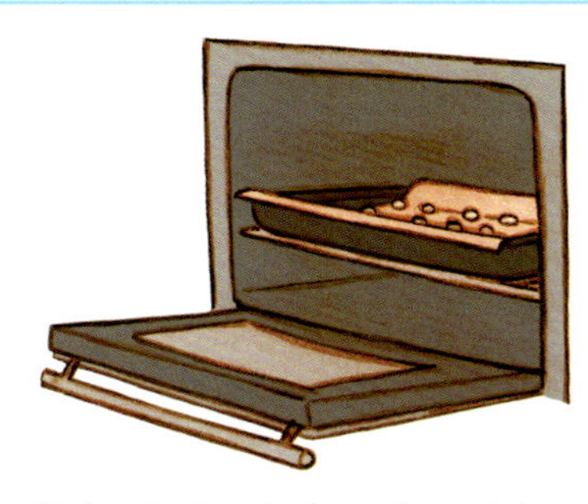

6 Bake the beads for at least 3 hours, or until the dough has dried out, then leave to cool.

CRAFTY TIP:

You can choose what kind of dough or clay you use to make the beads. Read the opposite page to find out more.

7 Once the beads have cooled, use your paintbrush to apply paint to each bead.

8 Thread the wool through the end of the needle and tie a knot (about 5cm from the end of the wool).

9 Wiggle the needle through the beads so that they fall to the knotted end.

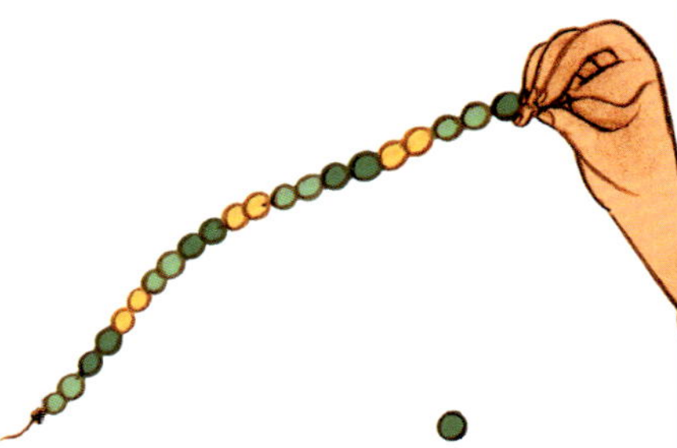

10 Keep filling the necklace with the beads until you have 1 bead left (and about 5cm of wool at the end). Put that bead to the side.

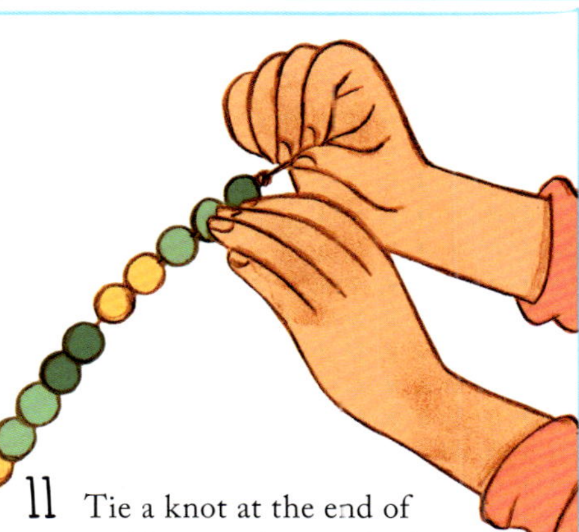

11 Tie a knot at the end of the necklace as close to the last bead as possible.

12 Thread the remaining bead onto the very end of the wool, then tie in place. This will form a clasp to fasten the necklace.

13 Make a little loop in the other end of the wool so that it fits snugly over the final bead, then knot in place.

CHOOSE YOUR DOUGH!

Clay beads: Roll air-drying clay into little beads, make a hole in each, then leave the clay to dry. Paint with poster paint, leave to dry, then varnish with a little PVA glue for extra shine.

Pre-dyed salt dough: Add a couple of drops of food colouring to the dough mixture at step 2 to make dough that already has some colour in it.

Pasta beads: Penne pasta shapes are perfect for threading onto a necklace as they are tube-shaped and hard-wearing. You can also paint them.

FRIENDSHIP BRACELETS

YOU WILL NEED:

1 cardboard toilet roll

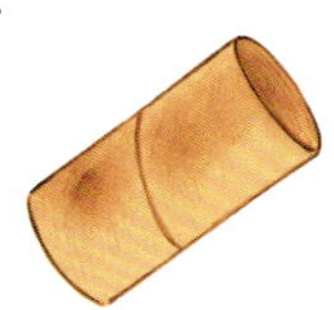

Scissors

7 long strands of coloured embroidery thread (each strand at least 50cm long)

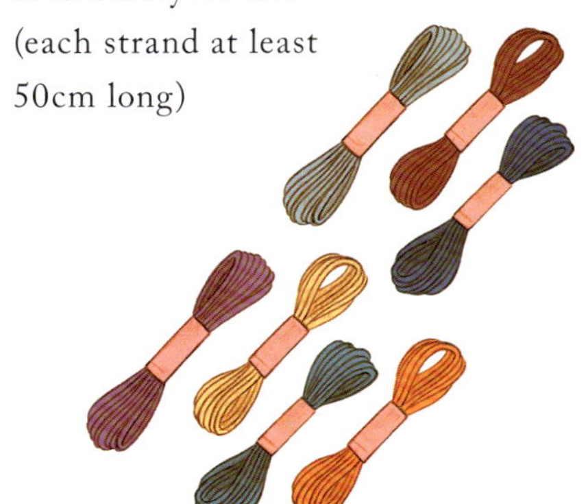

For this activity, we are once again using a leftover cardboard toilet roll to create something beautiful. This time, once you've finished weaving colourful threads around the toilet-roll template, you'll be left with a braided bracelet that you can give as a present to a special friend.

METHOD:

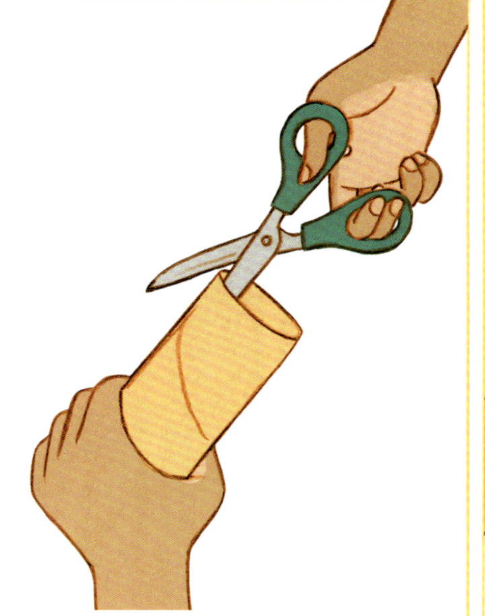

1 Cut a 1cm slit in the top of your tube, then another facing it.

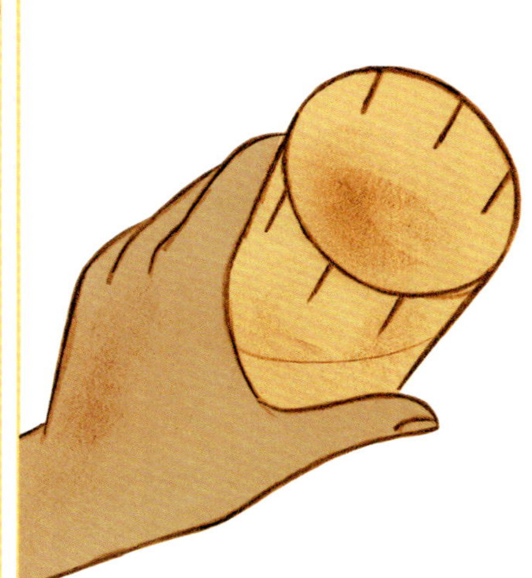

2 Cut 1 slit in between each notch, then 4 more in between those, so that you have 8 evenly spaced slits altogether.

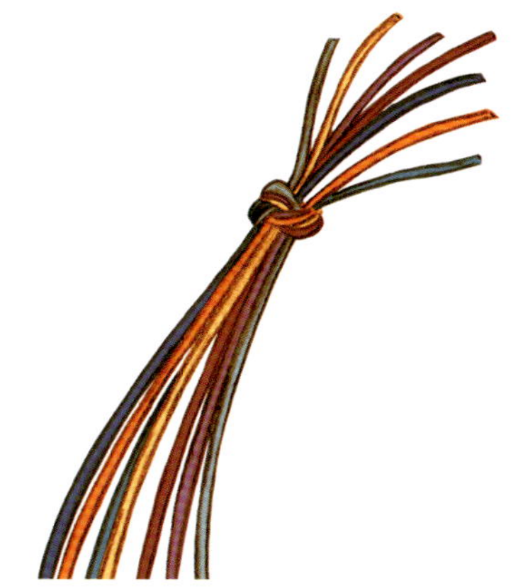

3 Gather the strands of thread together neatly, then tie a knot in the top, leaving about 5cm from the knot to the ends of the threads.

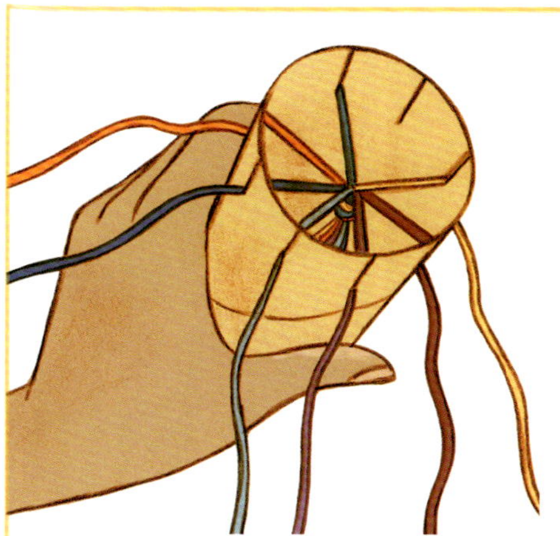

4 Put the knotted end into the centre of the tube, then separate out each strand, wiggling 1 strand into each slit in the tube, until you are left with 1 empty notch.

CRAFTY TIP:

Make sure to measure the length of thread really carefully so that the bracelet fits your friend's wrist.

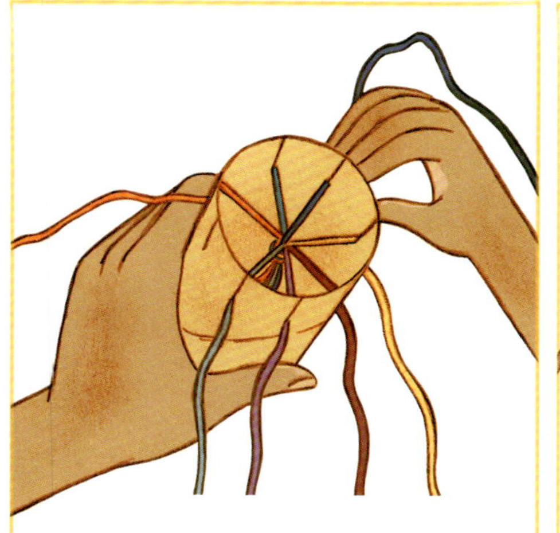

5 Find the strand of thread that is 3 notches away from the empty slit and bring it down into the empty slit. Try to keep your threads quite taut as you braid them.

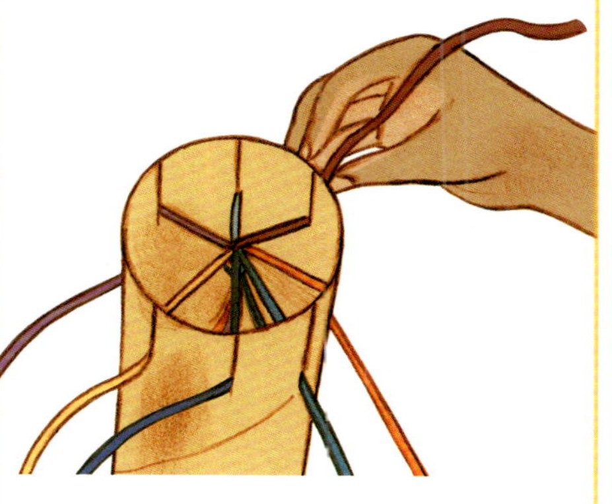

6 You will now have an empty slit where the strand was previously. Rotate the tube so that the empty slit is facing you. Take the strand of thread that is 3 notches away from the empty slit and bring it down into the empty slit.

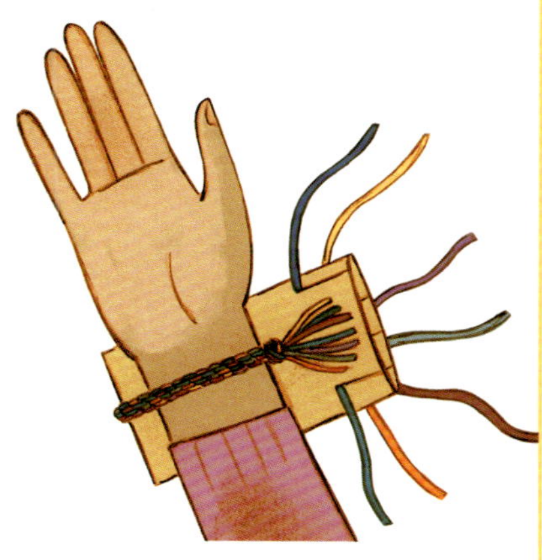

7 Repeat steps 5–6 until you make a length of braided strands that will fit your wrist. Make sure to braid more than you think (at least 3cm extra) – you don't want the bracelet to be tight.

8 Once you're happy with the length, wiggle the braid off the tube.

9 Bring the ends of the strands together, then loop them back over and under to make a secure knot.

10 Snip away the excess strands so that you have about 10cm of unbraided strands left.

11 Loop the 10cm of unbraided strands back towards the knotted end to create a large loop, then and tie in place.

Upcycled Photo Frame

You will need:

- An old photo frame (about 10cm x 15cm)
- 1 paper straw
- Scissors
- A pencil
- An old newspaper
- PVA glue
- A paintbrush
- 4 poster paints (choose your favourite colours)

Bring a tired-looking photo frame back to life with a little rolled-up newspaper, glue and paint. This is a great way to use leftover newspaper and give a frame a fun 3-D effect. Choose whichever colour paints you like, but try and make sure that the colours complement each other (turn to page 9 to find out more about colours).

Method:

1 Use a paper straw to measure the longest side of the frame, then use your pencil to mark the straw where the edge of the frame sits. Snip the end of the straw at the pencil mark so that your straw is the same length as the frame.

2 Roll newspaper into a tube the same length as the straw, making sure to keep it as tight as possible. Once you have a solid tube shape, stick it in place with a little tape, trim the ends with scissors, then ease it off the straw.

3 Repeat step 2 until you have enough newspaper straws to cover the longest sides of your frame.

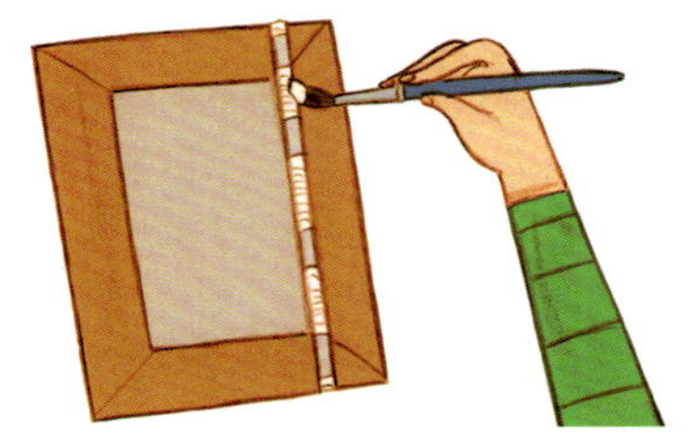

4 Apply PVA glue to the longest sides of the frame and stick the straws in place, adding glue in between each straw to make sure they stick.

5 Once the longest sides are done, take your straw and use it to measure the empty space along the shorter edges.

6 Snip the end of the straw at the pencil mark and repeat steps 2–4 for the shorter edges.

7 Once your frame has been covered, carefully paint each line of rolled-up newspaper a different colour, using your poster paints (you may need to add 2 layers of paint).

8 Paint the dried frame with a final layer of PVA glue and leave to dry.

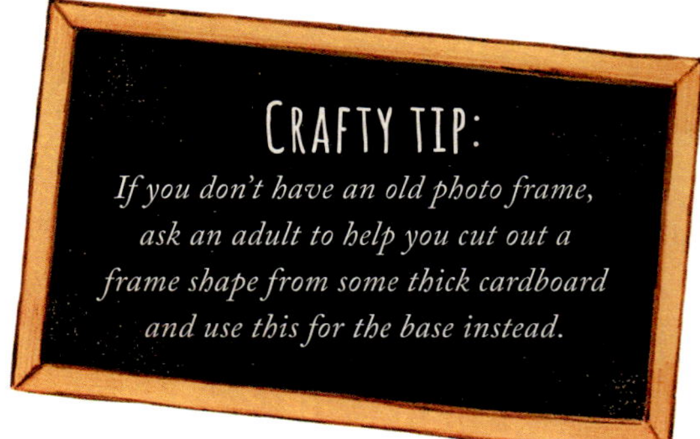

Crafty tip:

If you don't have an old photo frame, ask an adult to help you cut out a frame shape from some thick cardboard and use this for the base instead.

OUTDOOR ACTIVITIES

METAL WINDCHIME

YOU WILL NEED:

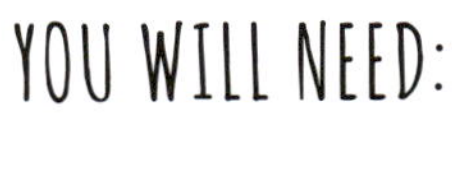

A 30cm-long stick

A ruler

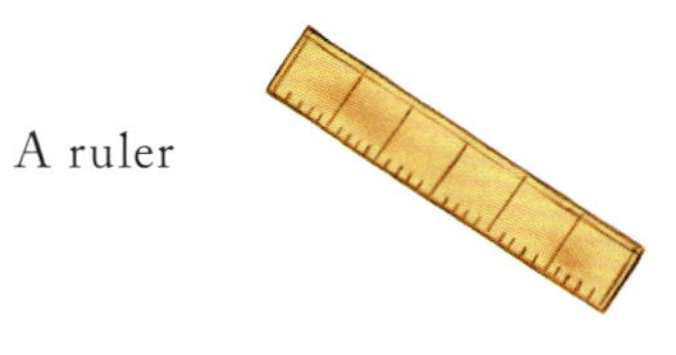

Scissors

A reel of gardening twine

6 small metal objects (keys, padlocks or teaspoons)

Windchimes can be made from scrap-worthy materials that create amazing sounds when jangling in the wind. For this activity, we're going to use old metal keys, padlocks and cutlery – just make sure they aren't sharp or too heavy!

METHOD:

1 Find a stick in your garden (or outdoors) that is about 30cm long.

2 Use your ruler to measure (and your scissors to cut) 3 shorter lengths of twine (each measuring 20cm) and 3 longer lengths of twine (each measuring 30cm).

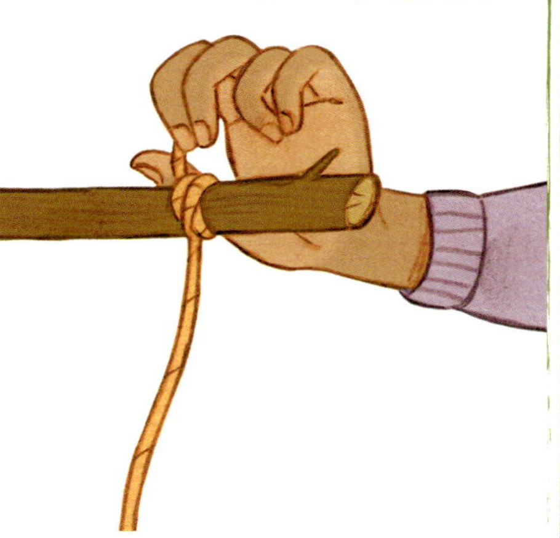

3 Loop 1 of the 20cm lengths of twine over the far end of the stick (about 2.5cm from the end) and knot to fasten it in place.

4 Loop 1 of the 30cm lengths of twine over the stick (about 5cm along from the first knot) and knot in place.

5 Repeat steps 3–4 until you have 6 alternating lengths of twine, hanging all along the stick.

6 Tie 1 small metal object to the end of each length of twine.

7 Cut a 40cm length of twine. Attach it just before the first bit of knotted twine on the end of the twig.

8 Loop this length of twine to the other end, just after the last bit of knotted twine, and secure in place. This will be your hanger.

9 Pick up your windchime, using the hanger, and ask an adult to help you hang it over a nearby tree or metal bracket.

10 When the wind blows, listen out for the metal objects tinkling together in the breeze.

GET FORAGING!

If you can't find scrap metal objects at home, take a look in your garden for some nature inspiration! Bamboo canes are hollow and make a great sound when knocked together. Nuts and shells you find outdoors will also make great sounds on your windchime.

TEACUP BIRD FEEDER

YOU WILL NEED:

1 teacup and matching saucer

A glue gun (or 1 tube of superglue)

A reel of gardening twine

A handful of birdseed

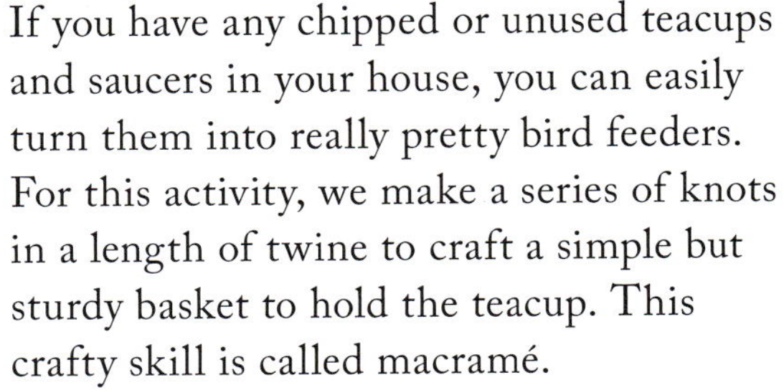

If you have any chipped or unused teacups and saucers in your house, you can easily turn them into really pretty bird feeders. For this activity, we make a series of knots in a length of twine to craft a simple but sturdy basket to hold the teacup. This crafty skill is called macramé.

METHOD:

1 Ask an adult to help you find an unused or chipped teacup and matching saucer that you can use for this project.

2 Ask your adult to pipe a circle of hot glue (or superglue) onto the ring of the saucer and the base of the teacup.

3 Carefully stick your cup onto the saucer so that it fits snugly into the groove. Push it down to make the glue stick, then leave to set.

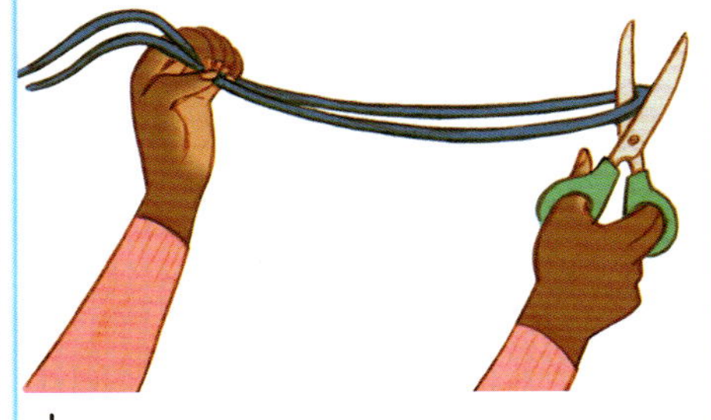

4 Spool out a 4m length of twine. Cut the twine in half so that you have 2 equal lengths.

5 Fold 1 length of twine in half to form 1 big loop. Holding the twine in the middle, pinch the ends together with your other hand. Feed the ends through the first loop to form a second loop.

6 Put the loop over the teacup and pull the ends of the twine until the loop sits tightly around the base of the cup. Secure in place with a knot.

CRAFTY TIP:

If you can't find a teacup and saucer at home, ask an adult to look out for one at a charity shop and upcycle it into this bird-friendly project.

7 Repeat steps 5–6 with the second length of twine, fastening the second loop at the opposite side of the teacup so that you have a length of twine hanging on either side of the cup.

8 Take 1 loose length from each side of the cup, bringing them together halfway up the side of the teacup. Tie them together with a little knot.

9 Turn the cup around and repeat step 8 with the untied lengths from each side of the cup.

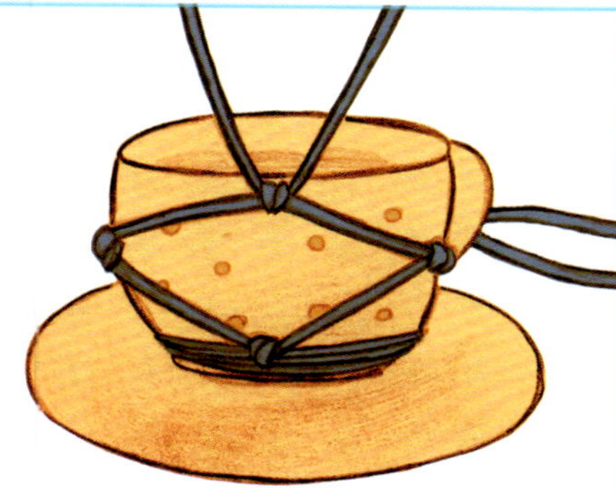

10 Repeat steps 8–9 once more, this time tying the twine together so that it sits further towards the top of the cup.

11 Gather all the lengths of twine together and tie a knot at the top.

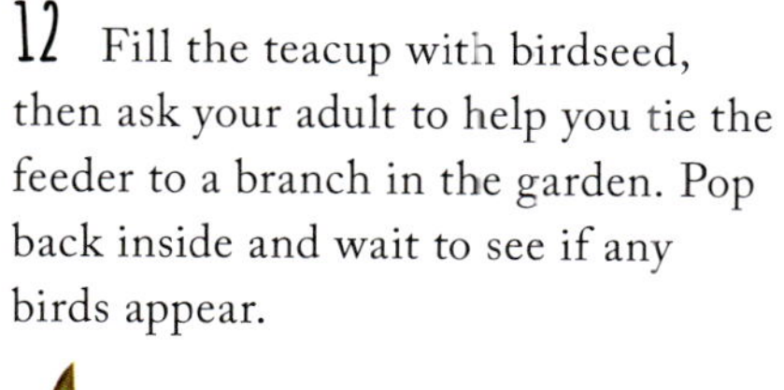

12 Fill the teacup with birdseed, then ask your adult to help you tie the feeder to a branch in the garden. Pop back inside and wait to see if any birds appear.

MAKE A BEAUTIFUL BIRD BATH!

Follow steps 1–11 of the instructions above, then fill your teacup with a little water – the perfect way to offer a safe bath for birds in your garden. You can even add chopped fruits and berries to the saucer for a truly decadent treat!

WIRE WINDOW STARS

YOU WILL NEED:

A pair of gardening gloves

A reel of green gardening wire

Scissors

A reel of gardening twine

1m string of fairy lights (battery-operated)

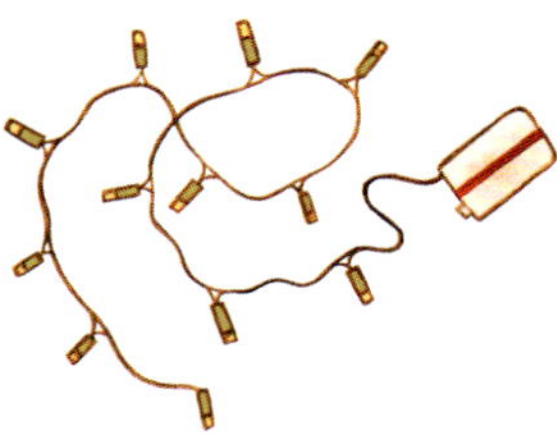

Metal is used in so many household things. From tiny wires in a plug to metal that makes a simple clothes hanger, it is a very useful material. For this activity, you will need metal wire that is thin and pliable, which means something that will bend easily. Gardening wire is nice and bendy and is coated in a protective layer, making it a little easier to work with.

METHOD:

1 Put on your gardening gloves. Ask an adult to help you spool out and cut a 40cm length of gardening wire.

2 Carefully bend the wire into a triangle shape that has sides that are each about 10cm long, but leave an extra 5cm at each end of the wire.

3 Pinch together the ends of the wire and twist together to hold your triangle shape in place.

4 Repeat steps 1–3 to make another triangle shape.

5 Place 1 of the triangles on a flat surface so that the twisted point is facing away from you. Place the other triangle on top of the first so that the twisted point is facing towards you.

6 Cut 6 little lengths of gardening twine, and use them to tie a knot at the 6 points where the triangles overlap.

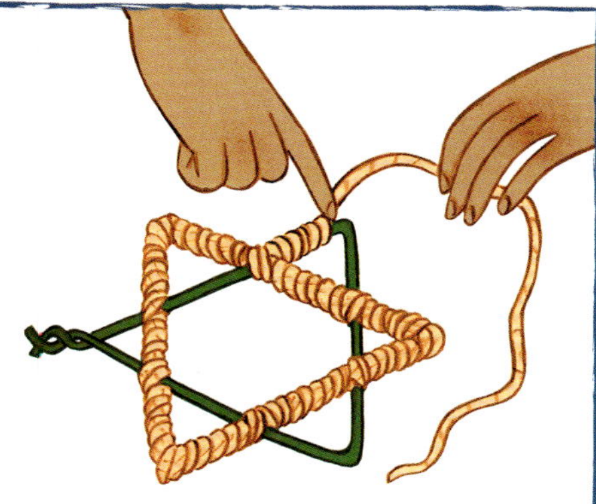

7 Once the star shape is secured in place, cut a long length of twine and wrap it around the top triangle, then the bottom triangle, until the entire star shape is covered in twine.

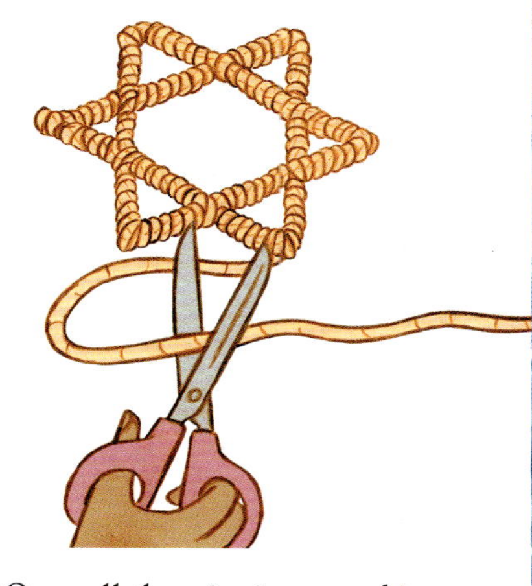

8 Once all the wire is covered in twine, leave about 10cm of extra twine at the end, then snip away any excess.

9 Loop the extra twine around and under the top of the star and tie in place to make a little loop.

10 Repeat steps 1–9 to make 8 stars.

11 Cut out a 1m length of twine, then thread the loops of the stars along it.

12 Weave the length of fairy lights along the long piece of twine, looping them up and around each star.

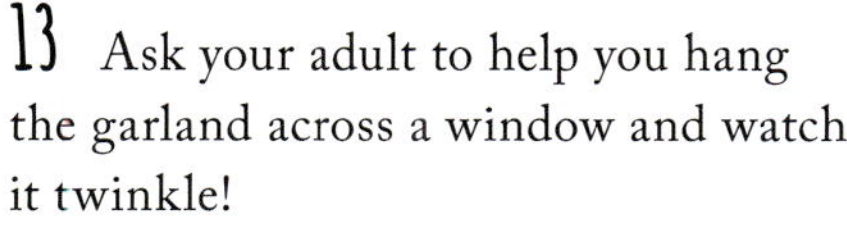

13 Ask your adult to help you hang the garland across a window and watch it twinkle!

CRAFTY TIP:

Always ask an adult to help with bending and shaping wire as the ends can be sharp and tricky to cut.

CRAFTY TIP:

If you don't have any gardening wire to hand, use pipe cleaners instead!

COLOURFUL CLAY VASE

YOU WILL NEED:

A 500ml empty plastic bottle (empty, clean and dry)

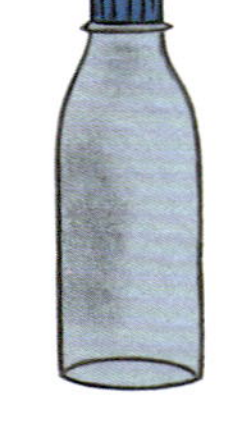

Scissors

A roll of masking tape

A 500g packet of modelling clay

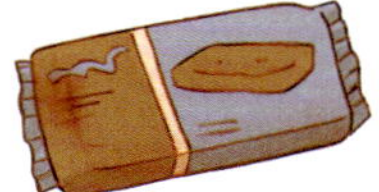

A wipe-clean chopping board

A pencil

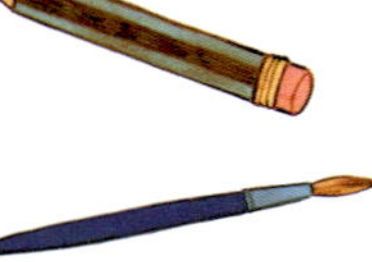

A paintbrush

6 poster paints (choose your favourite colours)

CRAFTY TIP:

Use mini stampers or even the end of a paintbrush to add pretty shapes to the clay coils.

Clay has been used for a very long time to make lots of items, from huge sculptures to small bowls. This handy material is easy to mould and sets hard once dried. For this activity, we use a classic technique called coiling. This is where you roll clay to make hooped shapes that are stacked on top of each other, giving the vase a solid structure and a pretty finish.

METHOD:

1 Ask an adult to help you cut the plastic bottle in half. The bottom half should be about 9cm high from the base to the top.

2 Ask your adult to stick tabs of masking tape around the cut end of the bottle to smooth off any sharp edges.

3 Recycle the top part of the bottle (with the lid) or pop it in your craft box, ready for another project.

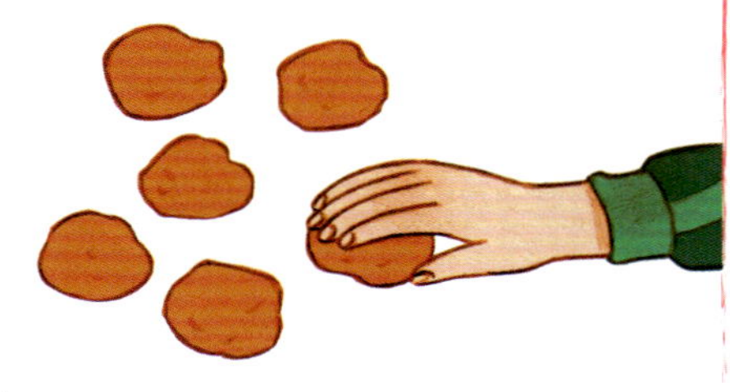

4 Open the packet of modelling clay and break off 6 golf-ball-sized pieces. Put any excess clay back into an airtight container.

5 Place the clay balls on your wipe-clean chopping board. Use your hands to roll each of the pieces into long sausage shapes that are about 2cm wide and 25cm long.

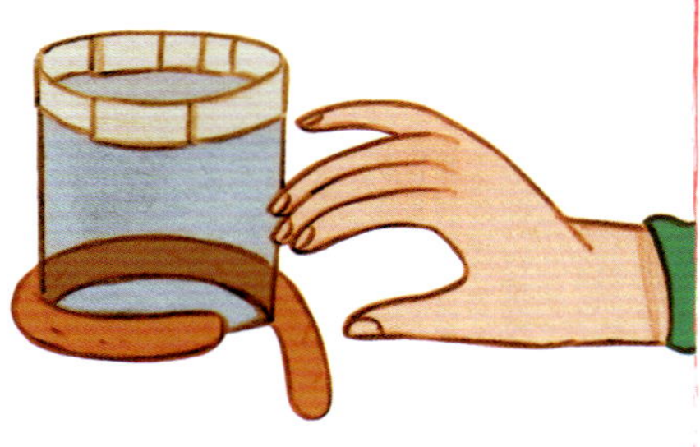

6 Starting at the bottom, coil 1 sausage-shaped piece of clay around the outside of the bottle.

7 Once the ends of the clay meet, break off any excess clay, then use your fingers to gently smooth the join.

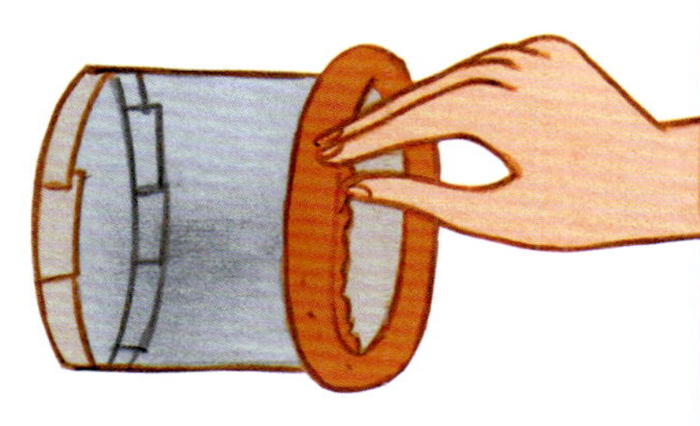

8 Use your fingers to pinch a little of the clay (about 2mm) under the bottle and smooth it down.

9 Push the bottle down gently onto the chopping board to make sure you have a nice seal on the clay.

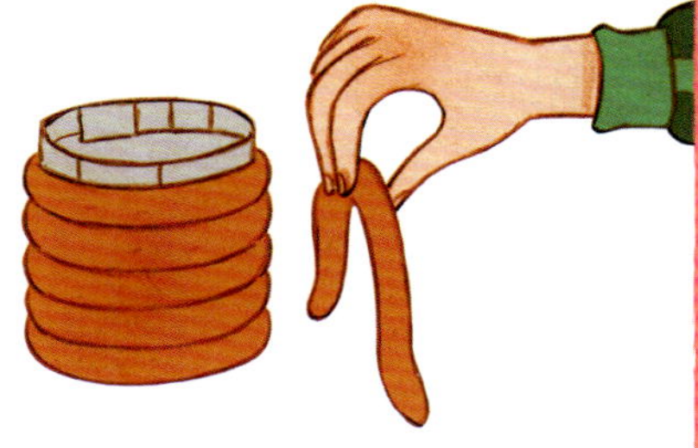

10 Repeat steps 6–7 until you have 6 coiled shapes stacked on top of each other (and the plastic bottle is concealed). If you need to, break a little more clay off from the packet to make a final coil.

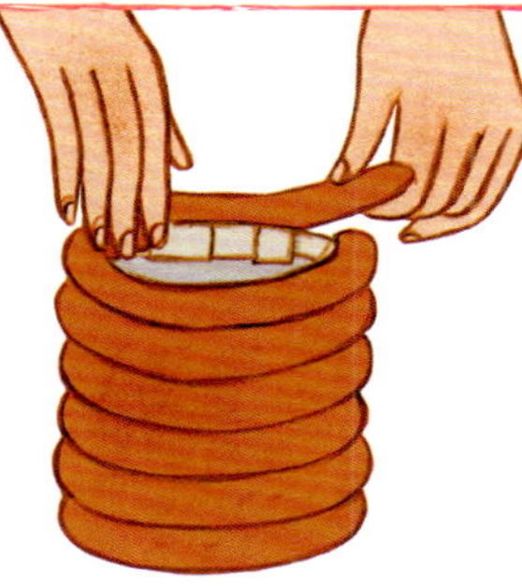

11 When you get to the last piece of clay, ask your adult to help pinch and smooth a little clay from the top of the coil over the rim of the plastic bottle.

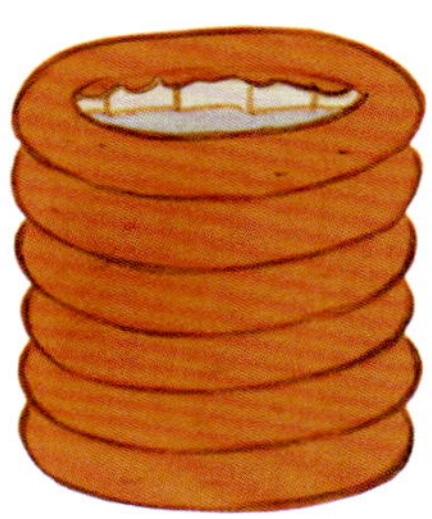

12 Leave your vase to dry. This will take at least 24 hours (check the packet's instructions for a guide) but it will be worth the wait!

13 Once the clay has dried, paint each hoop a different colour or create a fun design, then leave to dry.

14 Fill your vase with water and use it to display any cuttings from the garden.

CRAFTY TIP:

Dried clay is the perfect surface for painting on, which gives it a beautiful glossy finish.

Green garden wreath

You will need:

A dinner plate (about 25cm in diameter)

A piece of cardboard (at least 30cm x 30cm)

A pencil

A mug

Scissors

A reel of gardening twine

Dried leaves

Small twigs

Sprigs of rosemary

A 50cm length of ribbon

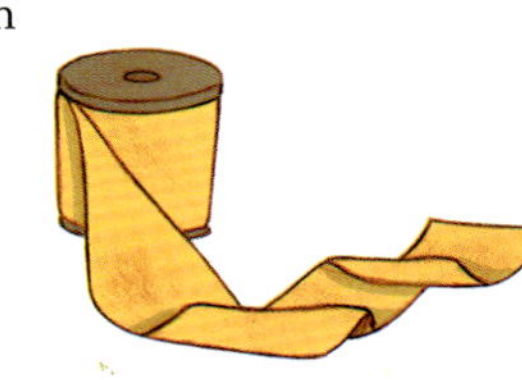

Wreaths are the perfect way to celebrate the outdoors and look beautiful when they are hung from a front door. Ask an adult to help you forage for twigs, dried leaves and sprigs of fresh herbs to add to your wreath.

Method:

1 Place the dinner plate on the cardboard and use a pencil to draw around it.

2 Place the mug in the centre of the circle and draw around it with a pencil.

3 Cut out the inner and outer circles from the cardboard so that you have a doughnut-shaped piece of cardboard.

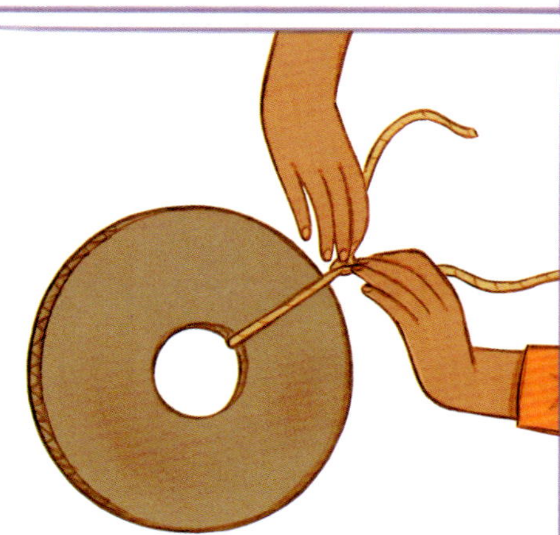

4 Loosen the reel of twine with your hands, then loop it around the circle, passing it through the hole and back over the edge of the wreath. Then tie a knot to secure it in place.

Crafty tip:

Loop short lengths of twine to the bottom of the wreath and tie extra foliage or little trinkets to the ends to add even more to your wreath.

5 Continue to loop the twine around the wreath, until the doughnut shape has about 20 loops spaced equally around it. The twine should sit snugly against the wreath.

6 When you get to your last loop, thread the end of the twine back under the loop and tie a knot to secure it in place, snipping away any excess.

7 Gather your leaves, twigs and rosemary sprigs. If you don't have any rosemary in the garden, ask an adult to help you find small green offcuts from a bush or a small tree.

8 Take a green offcut and gently wiggle it over and under the strands of twine to hold it in place. Work from the outside of the wreath to the centre, making sure that your foliage overhangs the edge.

9 Continue to add your nature cuttings to the wreath, adding as much or as little foliage as you would like.

10 When you're happy with your wreath, loop the ribbon through the hole and back over the top.

11 Gather the ends of the ribbon and tie them together in a bow.

12 Ask your adult to help you hang your wreath in the garden, indoors or even on your front door.

PRESSED-FLOWER BOOKMARK

When left to dry in the pages of a book, flowers become perfectly pressed petals ready to be used for craft activities! It takes 2–3 days for flowers to dry, but don't worry – it's worth the wait.

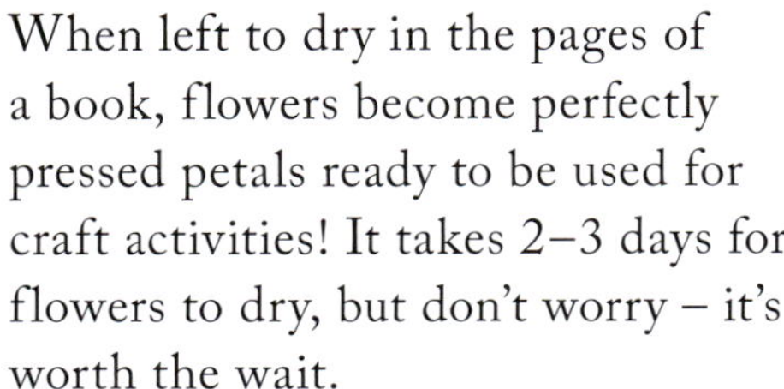

YOU WILL NEED:

A selection of 6 small flowers (heads and stems)

2 sheets of baking paper (about 20cm x 20cm)

2 heavy books

A small tray

1 A4 sheet of coloured card

A ruler

A pencil

Scissors

A paintbrush

PVA glue

A hole punch

A 20cm length of ribbon

METHOD:

1 Ask an adult to help you pick a selection of 6 small flowers (daisies are perfect). Make sure that the head of each flower is no bigger than 2cm; otherwise it will take a long time to dry.

2 Put 1 sheet of baking paper between the pages of a book. Lay your flowers on the paper, put another sheet of baking paper over the flowers, then close the book.

3 Add a heavy book on top and leave the flowers to dry. This may take 2–3 days, so get going with another craft activity while you're waiting.

4 Once your flowers have dried, carefully tip them onto a little tray and separate them out.

CRAFTY TIP:

Smaller flowers will dry faster and press a little flatter.

5 To make the bookmark, take your sheet of card and draw 2 rectangles that each measure 5cm x 15cm. Cut the rectangles out.

6 Use your paintbrush to paint PVA glue onto one of the pieces of card, then stick the other piece of card on top of it, making sure to align the edges.

7 Pop the card in the baking-paper-lined book, close and leave to dry.

8 Once the bookmark is firmly stuck together, remove it from the book. Use a hole punch to make a hole in the centre at 1 end of the card, leaving about 1–2cm from the top edge.

9 Use your paintbrush to paint the surface of the bookmark with PVA glue, then carefully pick up your flowers and press them onto the glue.

10 Leave the glue to dry a little so that the flowers are stuck in place. Paint the flower-sided bookmark with another layer of glue and leave to dry.

11 Loop the ribbon through the hole in the top of the bookmark and tie the ribbon in a knot.

Crafty tip:

Use wool or thread to create a pretty braided decoration for the top of your bookmark.

LEAF-PRINTED WINDMILL

YOU WILL NEED:

A square piece of paper (21cm x 21cm)

A pencil

A ruler

Scissors

A selection of fallen leaves

Orange, brown and green crayons (or 3 of your favourite colours)

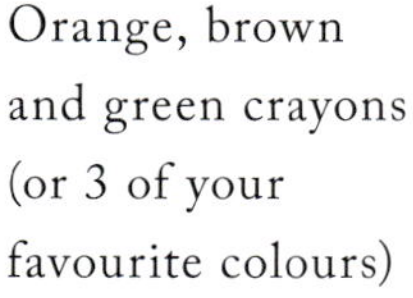

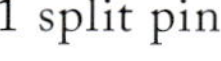

1 split pin

1 paper straw

Origami is an ancient art of paper folding to create 2-D and 3-D shapes. For this activity, we fold paper to create a windmill shape. To make it even more special, the paper is patterned with rubbings of leaves.

METHOD:

1 Ask an adult to help you find the centre of your square of paper and use your pencil to mark it with a dot.

2 Using a ruler and pencil, draw a line from the dot in the centre to a corner of the paper. Repeat for the other 3 corners.

3 Using your ruler, measure 16cm from 1 corner down the edge of the paper, then add a dot. Draw a curved line from the dot to the nearest diagonal line to make a petal shape.

4 Repeat step 3 until you have 4 of these shapes. Cut along the 4 curved lines so that you have 4 petals that are attached to the centre of the paper.

CRAFTY TIP:

Make more sheets of leaf-rubbed paper, then cut out little gift cards or gift tags.

5 Scatter the leaves onto a wipe-clean surface, then place your paper template on top.

6 Rub your crayons over the surface of the paper until the outlines and details of the leaves appear.

7 Once you're happy with your pattern, cut along the 4 lines from the corner to the centre of the paper, making sure to leave about 5cm from the pencil mark in the centre to the end of your cut.

8 Bring the pointed end of each petal to the centre of the windmill, using your other hand to hold the petals in place.

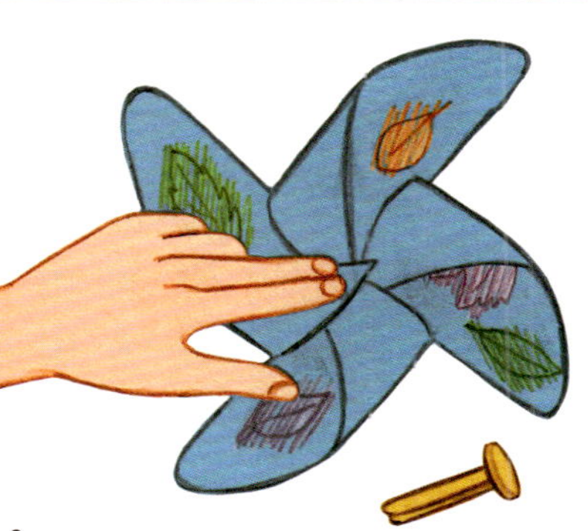

9 Once the pointed ends are all folded over to the middle, ask your adult to help you wiggle a split pin through the centre.

10 Push the pin through the top of the straw, then open up the pin to hold it in place. Make sure to leave room between the back of the windmill and the straw so that the windmill will turn.

11 Pop the windmill in a flower pot, or on a windowsill and watch as it turns in the wind.

Windmill garland

1. Make 6 leaf-printed windmills (up until step 9).
2. Cut out a 1m length of wool.
3. Take 1 of the windmills and fasten it to the end of the wool using the split pin.
4. Continue to attach your windmills to the wool, spacing them out evenly.
5. Ask an adult to help you hang up your garland!

PAINTED PEBBLE BEE

Pebbles are a beautifully smooth surface for painting on. Once you've finished your pebble, hide it in the garden and see if your friends or family can find it. Draw a treasure map to help them find the pebble!

YOU WILL NEED:

- 1 smooth pebble
- A paintbrush
- Yellow, black and white poster paints
- 1 cold, used teabag
- A cup
- 1 A4 sheet of paper (scrap paper is perfect)
- 1 brown, washable felt-tip pen

METHOD:

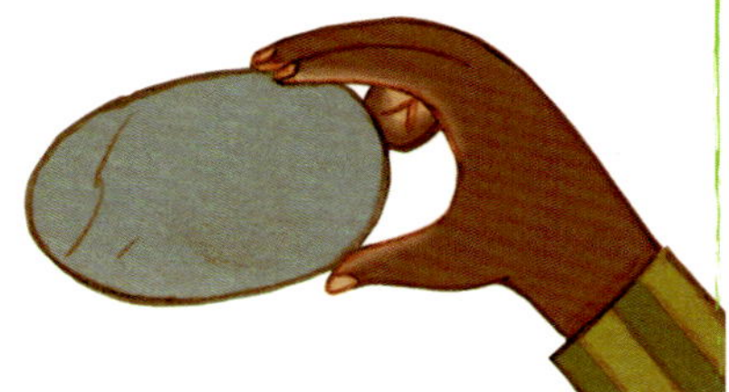

1 Find a smooth pebble or stone from your garden that has a large enough surface to paint an image on.

2 Paint yellow and black stripes along the pebble, adding a little black dot on the last yellow stripe for an eye, then leave to dry.

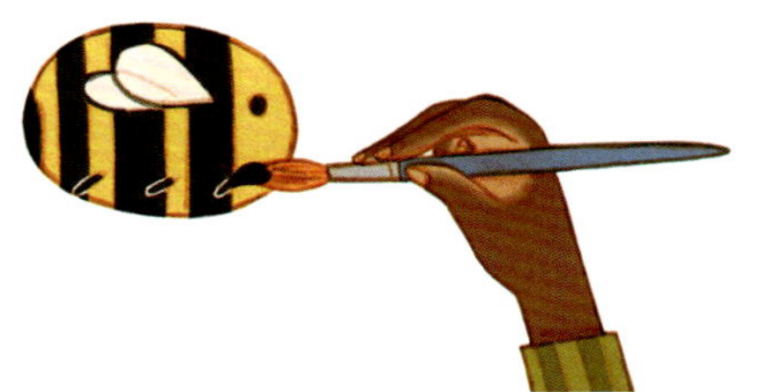

3 Paint on wings using white paint and little legs using black paint, then leave your pebble to dry again.

4 Ask an adult to help source a recently used, cold teabag that is still a little wet.

5 Brush the teabag over your sheet of paper, staining it brown, then leave the paper to dry.

6 Once your paper is dry, tear the edges to make them look worn and tattered.

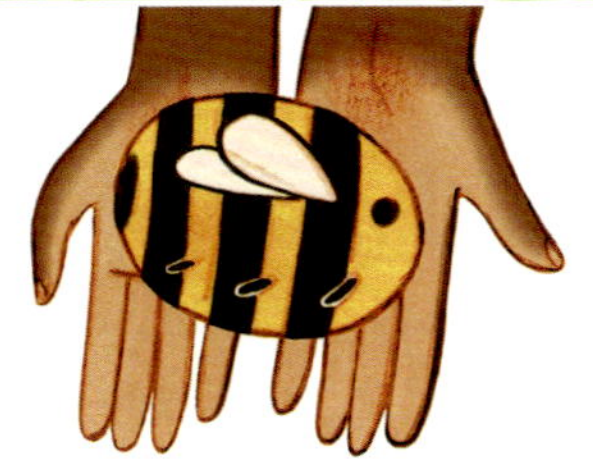

7 Hide your painted pebble bee in the garden.

8 Using your felt-tip pen, draw a simple map of the garden, marking a large "X" on the spot where the pebble is hidden.

9 Ask your friends and family to join in with the search.

CRAFTY TIP:

Use your painted pebble as a handy paperweight for storing tissue or paper.

PEBBLE DESIGN IDEAS

Pebble bugs: Creepy crawlies come in all shapes, sizes and colours. Paint a spotty ladybird, a leggy millipede or even a spooky spider on your pebble.

Pebble namesakes: Paint the name of your friend or family member on a pebble. Decorate it with painted flowers or stars and give it to them as a gift.

You will need:

- 1 A4 sheet of paper
- A pencil
- Scissors
- 1 medium-sized terracotta plant pot (about 20cm high)
- A roll of sticky tape
- A paintbrush
- Green, yellow and black poster paints

Sunflower-stencil flowerpot

Use this simple sunflower template to create a pot that will look beautiful in your garden or on a windowsill. Once your pot is painted, ask an adult to help you add soil and plant a sunflower seed, then wait for your flower to grow, grow, grow!

Crafty tip:
Press the paint onto the stencil with a sponge to give an interesting texture to your painting.

Method:

1 Fold your sheet of paper in half, then in half again. Open it back out, then cut down the fold lines so that you have 4 smaller pieces of paper.

2 Draw the outline of the head of a sunflower on 1 of the pieces of paper, leaving a 3cm border around the drawing.

3 Draw the outline of a leaf on 1 of the pieces of paper, leaving a 3cm border around the drawing.

4 Once you're happy with your outlines, ask your adult to help you make a snip in the centre of the design and cut around the pencil edges so that you are left with 2 templates.

5 Wrap your sunflower template around the plant pot (just below the rim), and stick it snugly in place with tape.

6 Brush yellow paint over the stencil, making sure that the gap where the flower design sits is filled with colour.

7 Carefully peel away the template, turn your pot around, then repeat steps 5-6 to add 4 sunflower stencils, evenly spaced, around the side of the pot.

8 Paint a green line from the bottom of each flower head to the bottom of the pot. When the lines have dried, stick your leaf stencil in place next to each line and dab with green paint.

9 Once the paint has dried, add little dots of black paint to the centre of each flower, then paint green and yellow stripes along the lip of the pot and leave to dry.

Nature Collage

You will need:

- A selection of fallen leaves, grass and small flowers
- 1 A3 sheet of craft paper
- A paintbrush
- Green, brown, yellow and red poster paints (or 4 of your favourite colours)
- PVA glue

Collage involves sticking different types of material onto a sheet of card or canvas to make a vibrant image. You can use photographs, textured paper or even fabric to create a collage. For this activity, we are going to forage in the garden for your materials! Search for dried leaves, grasses and small flowers to make your very own nature collage.

Method:

1 Ask an adult to help you find a selection of fallen leaves, grasses and small flowers to stick onto your collage. Try and find things that have interesting textures, colours or shapes.

2 Lay out your craft paper on a wipe-clean surface.

3 Paint a selection of shapes, lines and images on the paper using your paintbrush and paints. You can dip a leaf in the paint and press it onto the paper to make a stamp. Be as imaginative and creative as you like!

4 Once you're happy with your painting, leave the painted paper to dry in the sun and start to spread your cuttings out on a tray.

5 Place the cuttings on the craft paper. Try to space them out so that there is room between them and you can still see some of the paint patterns underneath.

6 Start to glue the cuttings down onto the paper with a little PVA glue.

7 If you'd like to, add more paint to the collage – you can even use your paintbrush to brush some paint on top of the stuck-down cuttings.

8 Once you're happy with how it's looking, leave your collage to dry in the sun, then ask an adult to help you stick it up in your room.

DO-IT-YOURSELF DECORATIONS

MINI FELT BUNTING

YOU WILL NEED:

3 pieces of coloured felt (each about 10cm x 20cm)

A small ruler

A fabric pen

Scissors

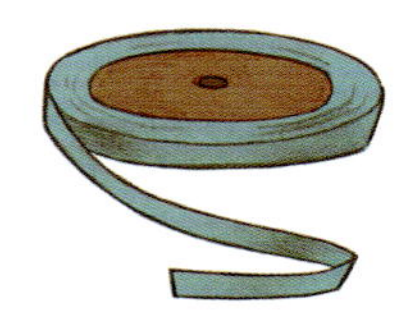

A hole punch

A 1m length of ribbon (0.5cm wide)

Bunting looks beautiful and is so much fun to make. You can hang it in a window, weave it around a bedframe or string it across a door to brighten up a small space. Because the bunting triangles are quite small, you can use smaller scraps of old material for this project. Felt is perfect, as it is a strong fabric that a hole punch can cut through and it holds its shape nicely.

METHOD:

1 Starting at the corner of one of the pieces of felt, use your ruler to measure out a 5cm horizontal line and draw the line on the fabric using your fabric pen.

2 Find the middle of the 5cm line, and add a dot with your pen, then draw a vertical 5cm line from this point (this will be the top of your triangle).

3 Use your ruler and pen to add straight lines from the ends of the horizontal line to the top of the vertical line to make a triangle shape.

4 Repeat steps 1–3 until you have 5 triangles on the first piece of fabric. Then add 5 triangles to each of the remaining pieces of felt. Cut out the triangles so that you have 15 in total.

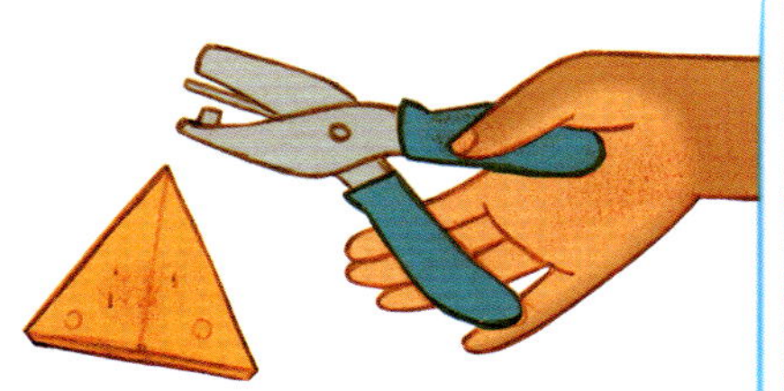

5 Ask an adult to help you punch a little hole into the top left-hand corner and top right-hand corner of 1 flag, using your hole punch.

6 Carefully wiggle the felt flag out of the hole punch and set aside. If you accidentally tear the felt, make another flag out of any leftover felt.

CRAFTY TIP:

Cut the sides of the bunting with crimped scissors to give each flag a pretty edge.

7 Repeat steps 5–6 until you have 15 hole-punched flags.

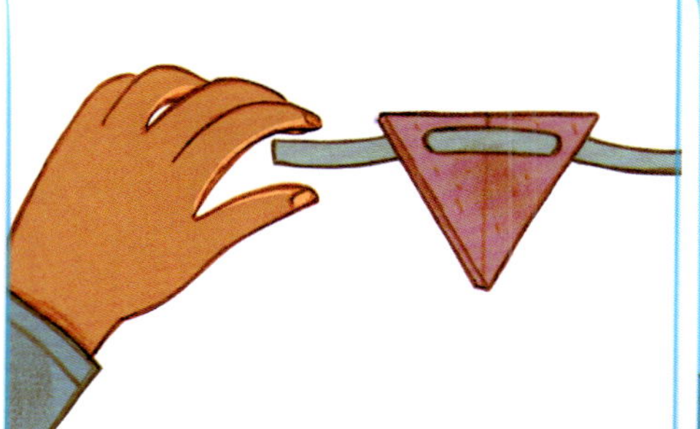

8 Once all of your flags have 2 holes, start to thread the ribbon through each flag so that it goes into one hole, round the back of the flag and up through the other hole.

9 Keep threading the flags onto the ribbon, alternating the coloured felt as you choose each flag.

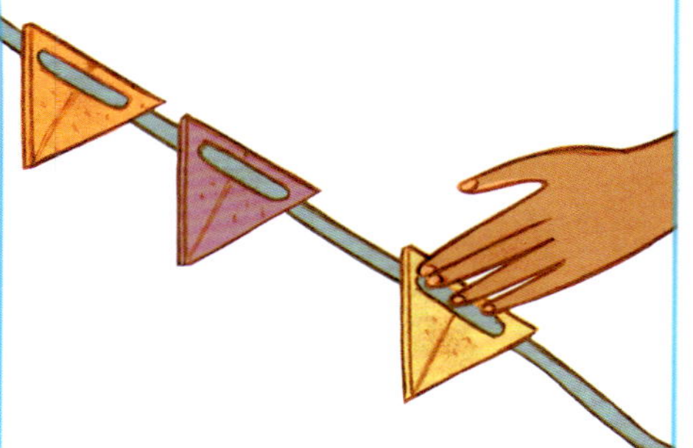

10 Push each flag along the ribbon so that they are evenly spaced along the entire length.

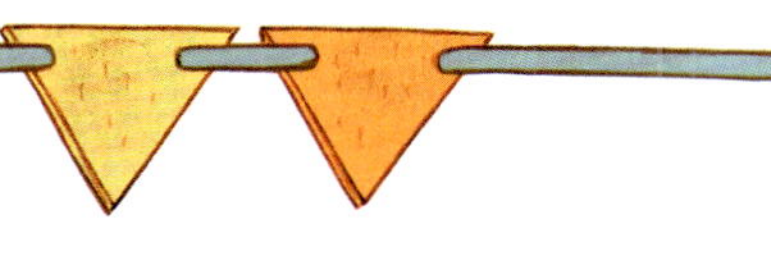

11 Keep moving the flags until you are happy with how they are arranged, leaving about 5cm from the last triangle to the end of the length of ribbon.

12 Use your fabric pen to add a letter, number or image to each flag. If you want to spell out your name, count the number of letters and try and place them in the centre of the bunting.

13 Ask your adult to help you hang your bunting in your room.

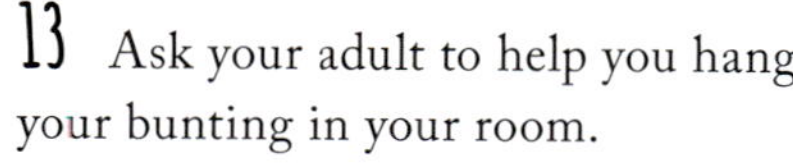

BUNTING BASED IDEAS

Cake-topper bunting: Cut out tiny triangle shapes from tissue or paper. Roll the widest end of the flag over some thread, then carefully stick in place with a little glue. Tie the ends of the thread to wooden kebab sticks, ready to be added to the top of a cake.

Get sewing: Put your sewing skills to the test! Ask an adult to help you sew pretty embellishments or patterns onto your bunting flags.

Paper bunting: If you don't have any material to hand, make the bunting flags from card, paper or even cardboard. Add a pretty finish with paint, collage or crayons and thread the flags onto the ribbon.

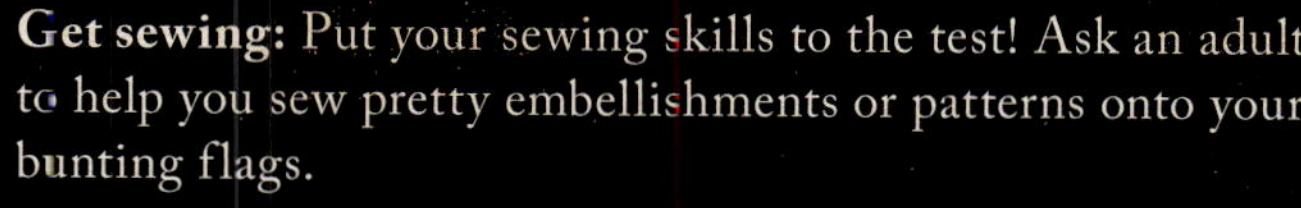

JAM-JAR TABLE LAMP

YOU WILL NEED:

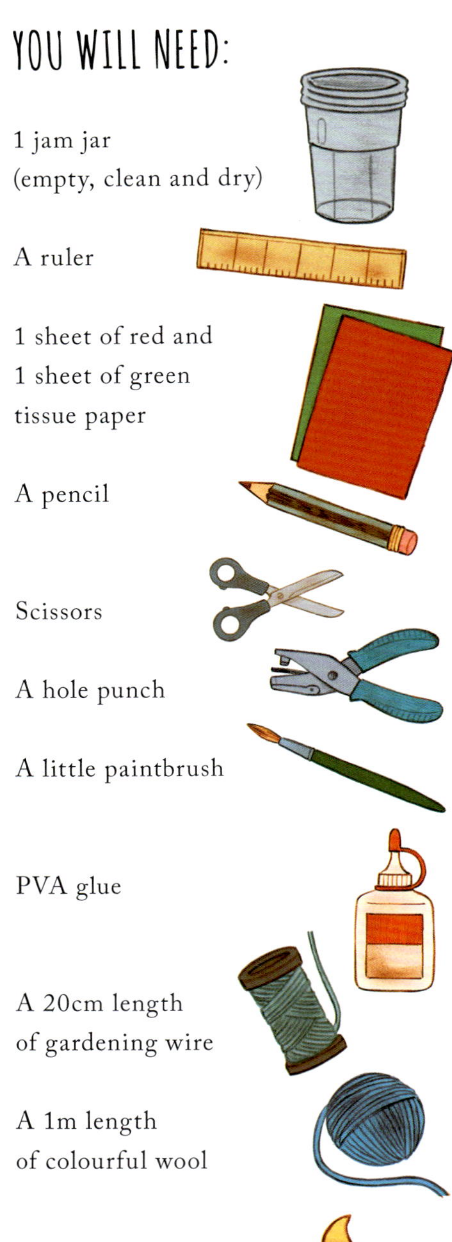

1 jam jar
(empty, clean and dry)

A ruler

1 sheet of red and
1 sheet of green
tissue paper

A pencil

Scissors

A hole punch

A little paintbrush

PVA glue

A 20cm length
of gardening wire

A 1m length
of colourful wool

1 LED tealight

Lamplight can brighten up a room and make it feel warm and cosy. For this activity, we upcycle a jam jar into a little lamp. The jar can be any size, but try to look out for one with pretty patterns or grooves. Before you start crafting, make sure your jam jar has been cleaned. Sticky jam and warm lighting do not make a good combo!

METHOD:

1 Take the lid off the jam jar and put it in your craft box.

2 Use your ruler to measure the height of the jam jar, from the base of the jar to just underneath the lip.

3 Unfold the red tissue paper. Use your ruler and pencil to measure the height of the jam jar. Add a pencil mark to the tissue paper where the height of the jar would sit.

4 Cut 2cm-wide strips of tissue from the edge of the tissue to the pencil mark. You will need about 6 strips in total.

5 Carefully punch a hole in the middle of each tissue strip, using your hole punch.

6 Repeat steps 2–5 with the sheet of green tissue paper, then carefully fold any leftover tissue paper back up and put it in your craft box.

CRAFTY TIP:

Put any leftover hole-punched tissue or trimmings into your craft box, ready for when crafting-inspiration strikes!

7 Paint a thin layer of glue onto your jar, using your paintbrush. Carefully stick a tissue strip vertically onto the jar – from under the lip of the jar to the base – taking care to smooth the tissue out to avoid any lumps.

8 Stick alternating strips of coloured tissue onto your jar, until it has been completely covered, then leave to dry.

9 Ask an adult to help you wrap the length of gardening wire around the rim of the jar.

10 When the wire ends meet, twist them round to secure the wire in place, then bend the rest of the wire over the top of the jar.

11 Wiggle the end of the wire back under the wire around the rim of the jar (on the opposite side) and twist in place to make a handle.

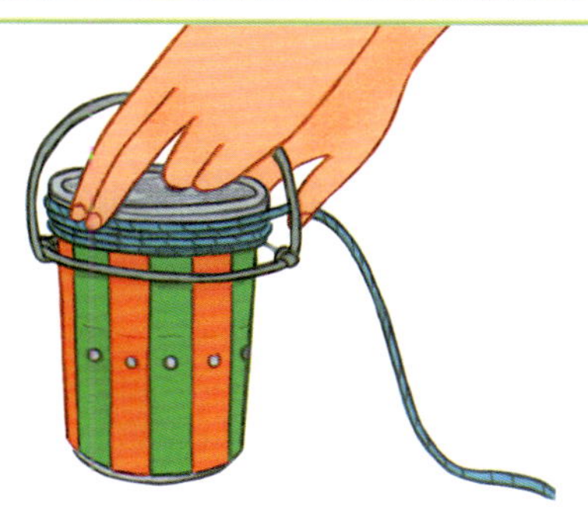

12 Wrap your wool around the top lip of the jam jar to cover the grooves in the glass where the lid was screwed on.

13 When you reach the end of your wool, tie it to the bottom of the wire handle.

14 Pop a little LED tealight in your jar, then ask your adult to help you hang it in place.

Decorative ideas

Glass paint: Ask an adult to help you paint pretty patterns onto your jar, using glass paint.

Shiny stick-ons: Stick shiny details like little sequins onto the outside of your jam jar.

Felt shapes: Create a 3-D edge to your lamp by cutting out little felt shapes and sticking them in place on the outside of the jar.

T-shirt cushion cover

You will need:

1 large, adult-sized T-shirt

Scissors

1 square cushion pad (about 40cm x 40cm)

A fabric pen

A ruler

Crafty tip:

Use a T-shirt with a striped or interesting pattern to make the cover look even more striking.

T-shirts are made out of soft and stretchy fabric – the perfect material for crafts. For this project, we're going to turn an old T-shirt into a beautiful cushion cover, with just a pair of scissors and your hands! And you get to upcycle a T-shirt that isn't worn any more and save it going to waste.

Method:

1 Ask an adult to help you cut along the 2 seams that run up the side of the T-shirt. Then cut along the seams from the neck to the edges of the sleeves. You should be left with 2 T-shirt-shaped panels.

2 Turn your T-shirt inside out, then place your cushion pad in the middle of 1 of the T-shirt panels.

3 Use your fabric pen to mark dots around the edge of your cushion pad. Put the cushion to the side, then use your ruler and pen to join the dots together to make a square shape.

4 Use your ruler to measure 5cm out from the corner edge of the square shape, then add a little dot with your fabric pen.

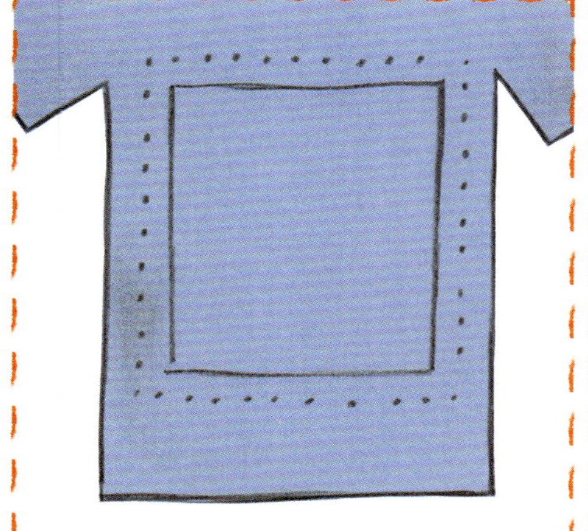

5 Continue to add dots that sit at 5cm intervals all along the edges of the first square shape.

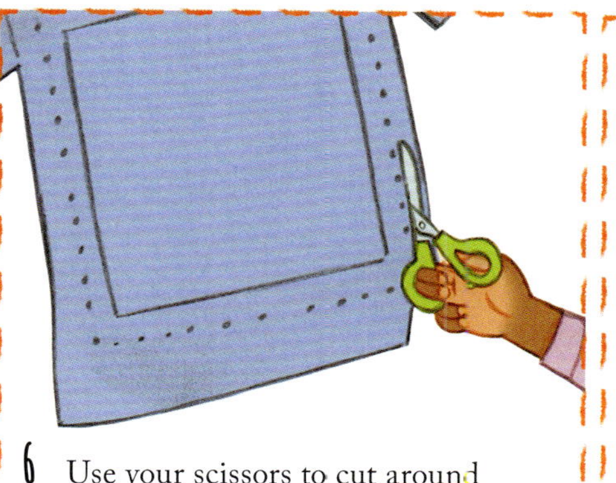

6 Use your scissors to cut around the dotted outline so that you have a square-shaped piece of fabric with a square sitting within it. Be careful to cut just outside of the dotted outline so that you can still see the dots.

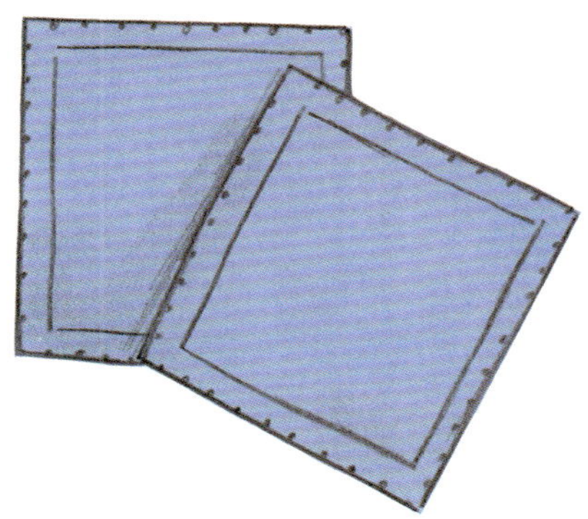

7 Repeat steps 2–6 to make a second square-shaped piece of fabric that is the same size as the first and also has a square sitting within a dotted outline.

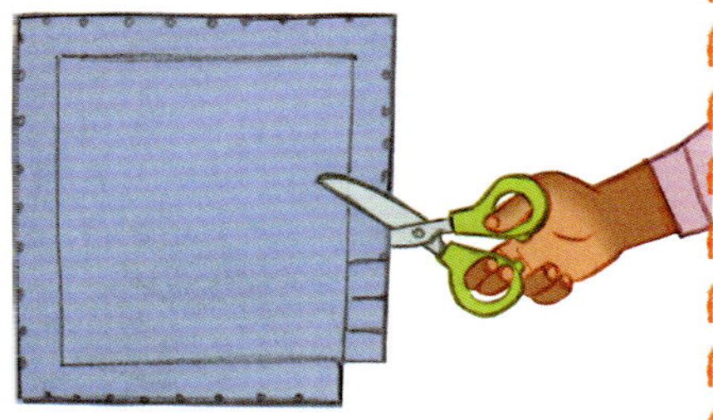

8 Ask your adult to help you snip from each dot at the edge of the fabric to the square-shaped outline so that you have 8 tabs around each edge (completely cutting away the tab from each corner).

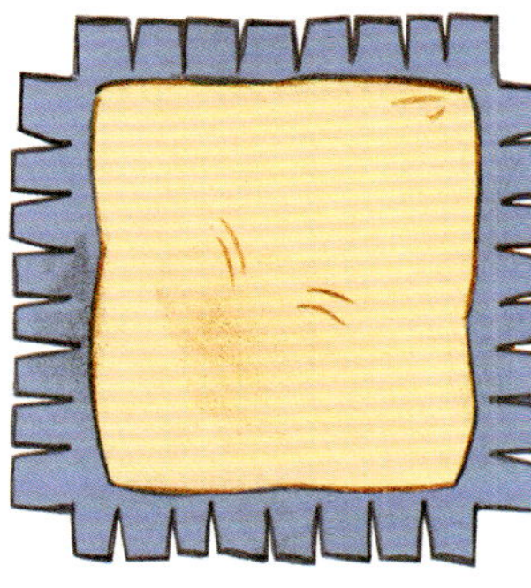

9 Repeat step 8 with the second piece of fabric, then lay this flat and place the cushion pad onto it.

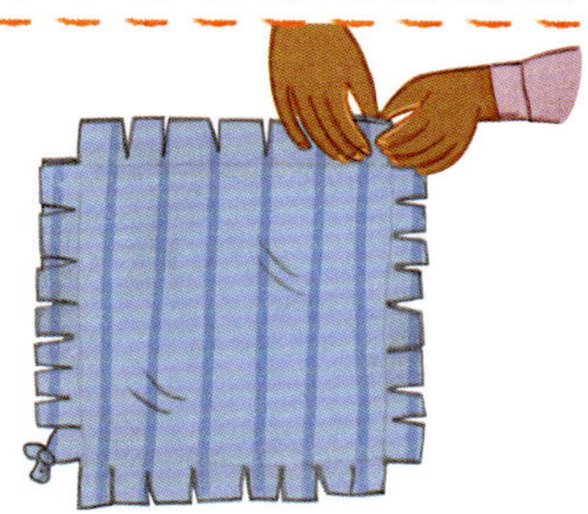

10 Lay the remaining piece of fabric on top, then gather 2 corresponding tabs at one corner of the cushion and tie them together with 2 knots to secure in place.

11 Keep tying the corresponding tabs together, working around the edges until the cushion pad is sealed.

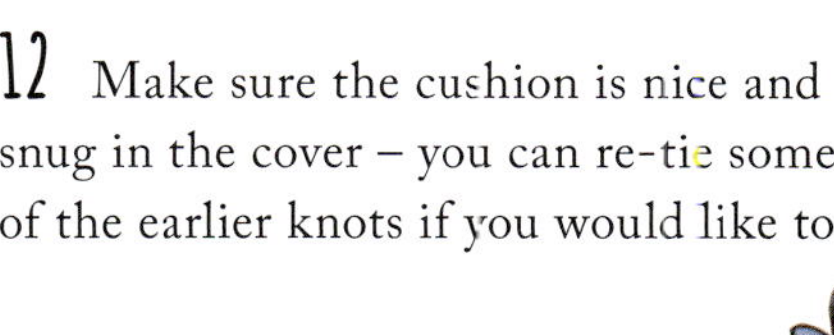

12 Make sure the cushion is nice and snug in the cover – you can re-tie some of the earlier knots if you would like to.

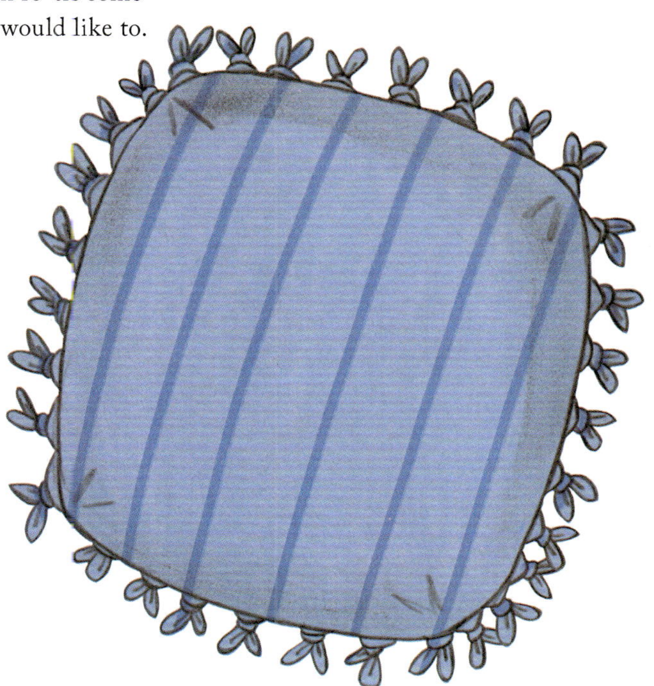

FELT MOSAIC COASTERS

YOU WILL NEED:

5 pieces of different-coloured felt (each at least 5cm x 2cm)

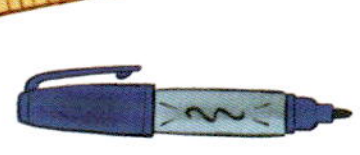

A ruler

A fabric pen

Scissors

A 10cm x 10cm square coaster

PVA glue

Felt is a lovely fabric to work with. It's thick and fuzzy and because it has lots of little fibres, it sticks really well together. It's also a chunky material, so is the perfect thing to protect a table from a wet cup. For this project, we upcycle an old coaster by sticking little felt tiles over it to create a felt mosaic.

METHOD:

1 Lay your 5 different-coloured pieces of felt out on a wipe-clean surface.

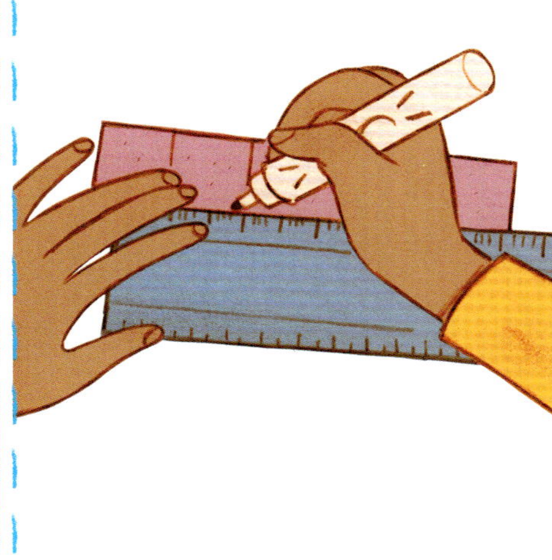

2 Use your ruler and fabric pen to mark out 5 squares (each measuring 2cm x 2cm) along each piece of felt.

3 Ask an adult to help you cut out all of the squares so that you have 25 little felt tiles.

4 Make sure that the underside of the coaster (sometimes made from cork) is facing down, then apply a little glue to a felt tile and stick it onto the top corner of the coaster.

CRAFTY TIP:

If you don't have any unused coasters to hand, ask an adult to cut out a small square of cardboard and use this as the base for your coaster.

CRAFTY TIP:

Choose whichever and however many colours of felt you like!

5 Keep filling your coaster with the little tiles, alternating colours as you go, so that you end up with a nice patchwork effect.

6 Try to make sure that the tiles fit tightly together as you stick them on. Once your coaster is full, leave it to dry for at least 1 hour.

7 When the coaster is dry, ask your adult to help you trim any excess felt away from the edges.

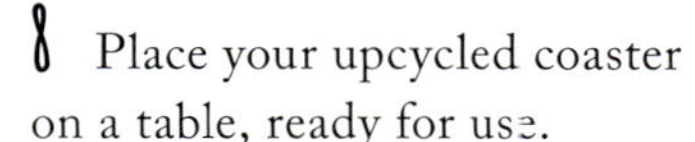

8 Place your upcycled coaster on a table, ready for use.

Crafty coaster ideas

Stripy coaster: Ask an adult to help you cut out strips of different-coloured felt that are about 1cm wide and 10cm long. Stick the strips side-by-side onto a coaster to make a stripy coaster.

Simply stuck: Put a mug onto a piece of felt. Ask an adult to help you draw around the base so that you have 2 circle shapes. Cut the felt circles out, then stick them together to make a simple coaster.

COAT-HANGER MOBILE

YOU WILL NEED:

2 wire coat hangers

A ball of wool

Scissors

4 little wooden pegs

4 small photos and 4 small objects or trinkets

A wire coat hanger is the perfect thing to make a light and pretty mobile for all of your memories. You can hang photos, drawings or even little objects from it. The beauty of a mobile is that you can keep updating it and adding new items like shells, buttons or even magazine cuttings.

METHOD:

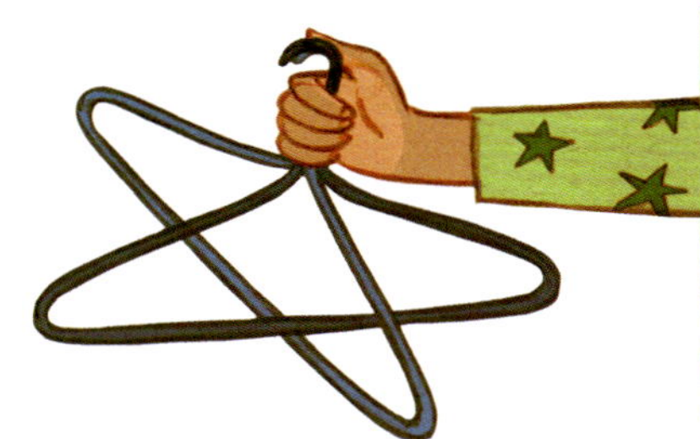

1 Ask an adult to help you find 2 wire coat hangers, then push one hanger through the other so that the tops meet in the middle and you have a cross shape.

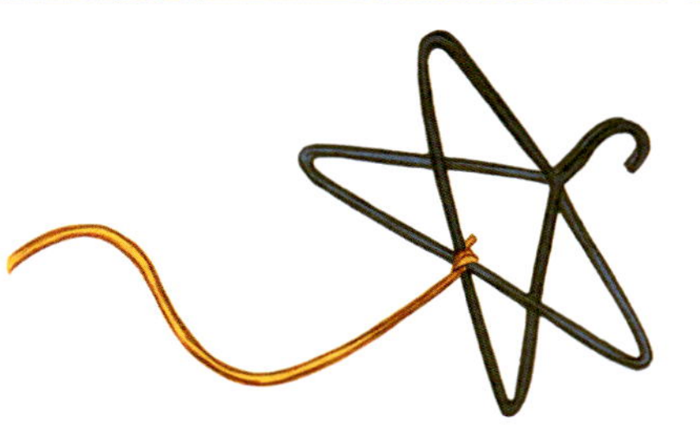

2 Ask your adult to help you cut away a long length of wool, then loop the end over the points where the hanger bases cross. Tie a knot to secure them in place.

3 Continue to loop the wool around and around, keeping it as tight as possible.

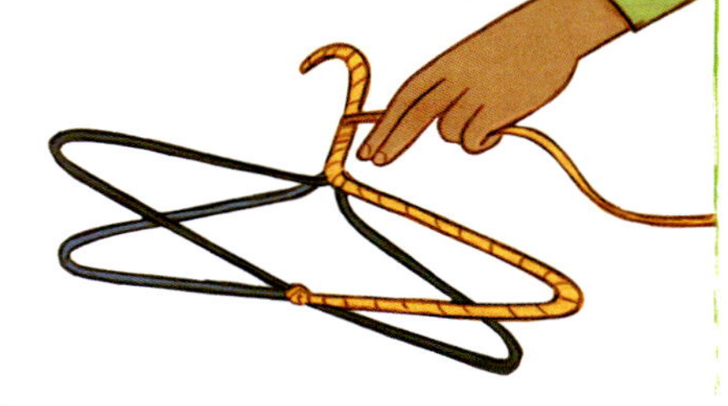

4 When you reach the top of the hangers, start to work back down the other side of the same hanger, wrapping a layer of wool around it.

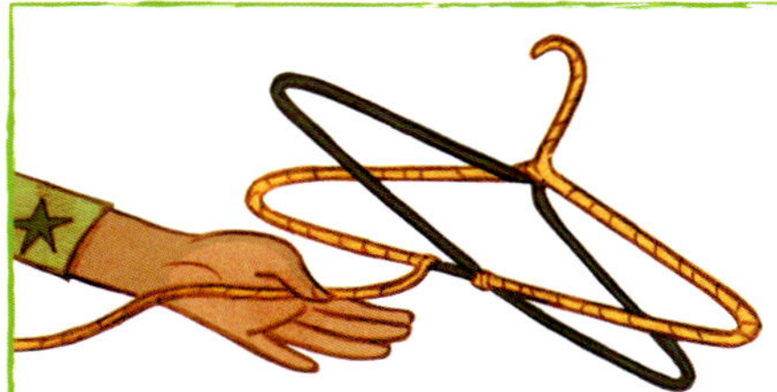

5 Continue to wrap the wool around the hanger until you reach the first point where you tied the knot. If you need more wool, tie a new length of wool to the end of the previous piece.

6 Tie another knot in the wool to secure it in place, then snip away any excess. You should now have 1 covered hanger and 1 exposed wire hanger.

7 Place your 4 wooden pegs along the exposed wire hanger, then attach a photo to each peg.

8 Ask your adult to help you cut 2 lengths of wool that are about 15cm long and 2 lengths of wool that are about 10cm long.

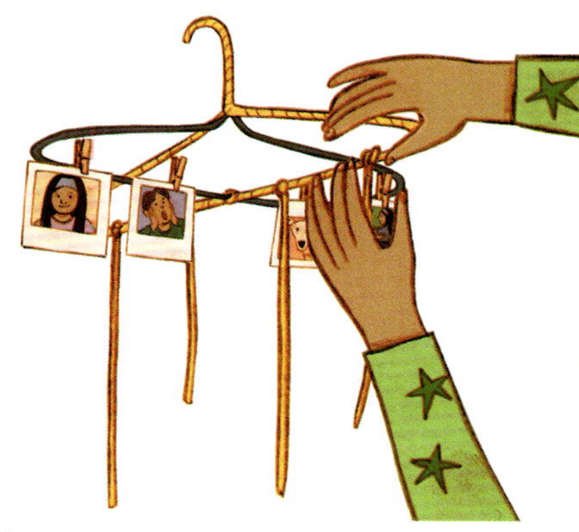

9 Tie each piece of wool to the woollen-covered hanger, alternating longer and shorter lengths and tying them at evenly spaced intervals.

10 Tie your trinkets to the end of each strand of wool.

11 Once you're happy with the mobile, ask your adult to hang it up in your bedroom.

CRAFTY TIP:

Ask an adult to help you wrap a small string of fairy lights around the top of your mobile to give it a warm glow.

Stamped Clay Door Hanger

You will need:

A 500g packet of modelling clay

A wipe-clean chopping board

A sheet of baking paper (about 30cm x 20cm)

A rolling pin

An 8cm round biscuit cutter

A ruler

A toothpick

A fork

A small paintbrush

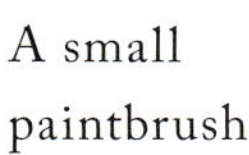

Blue and white poster paints (or 2 of your favourite colours)

A 20cm length of ribbon

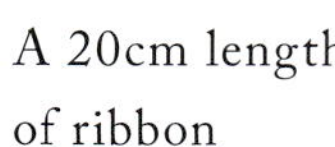

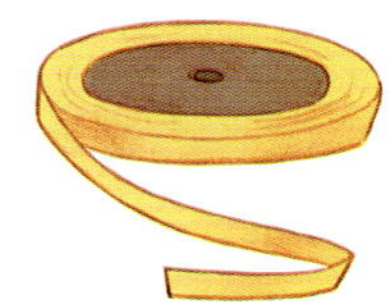

This stamped door hanger is perfect to hang on your bedroom door. We're using modelling clay for this project, but turn to page 39 to find out more about the different types of clay and dough that you can use.

Method:

1 Break off a big chunk of modelling clay (about 2cm x 6cm wide).

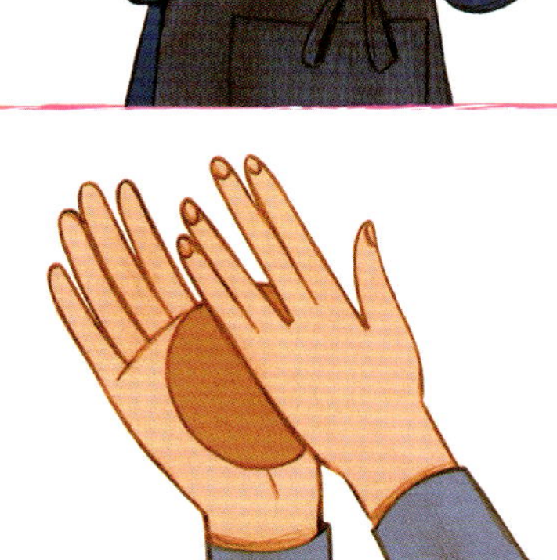

2 Roll the clay in your hands to make a ball. Then lay the clay ball on a chopping board lined with baking paper.

3 Use your rolling pin to roll the clay out until you have a disc that is about 10cm wide in diameter and 0.5cm thick.

4 Press your biscuit cutter quite hard into the clay, then wiggle it to cut out a circular-shaped piece of clay.

5 Put any excess clay back into the packet, ready for the next craft project.

6 Use a ruler to gently ease the disc off the paper, then place it back down – this is to stop it sticking to the paper as it dries.

Crafty tip:

Use whichever colour paint you like for this project. Turn to page 9 to find out more about mixing colours.

7 Using the toothpick, make a hole about 1cm from the top left-hand edge of the disc, then wiggle it until the hole is about 0.5cm big. Repeat on the right-hand side so that you have a hole on either side of the disc.

8 Use your toothpick to make deep dots in the clay to spell out a letter or a name. Wiggle the toothpick around to make the dots a little bigger.

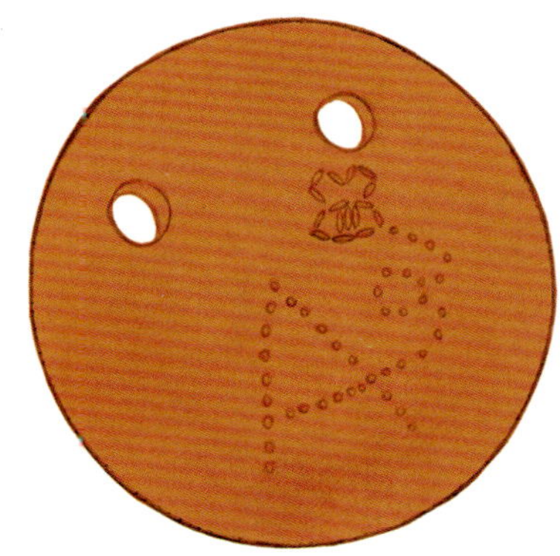

9 Use your toothpick to add pretty details around the clay, like flowers, stars or even a little bee and the trail it makes as it flies away.

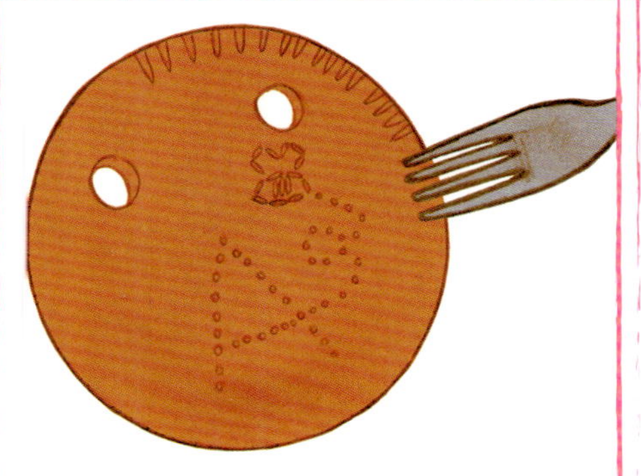

10 Press your fork around the edge of the clay disc to make a pattern.

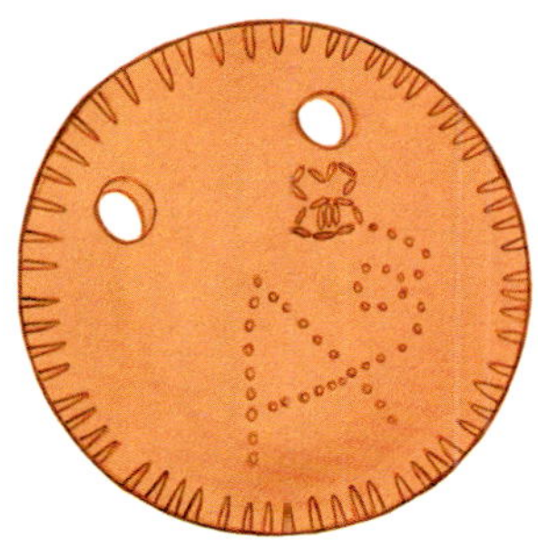

11 Leave your clay to dry. This will take at least 12 hours (check the packet's instructions for a guide) but it will be worth the wait!

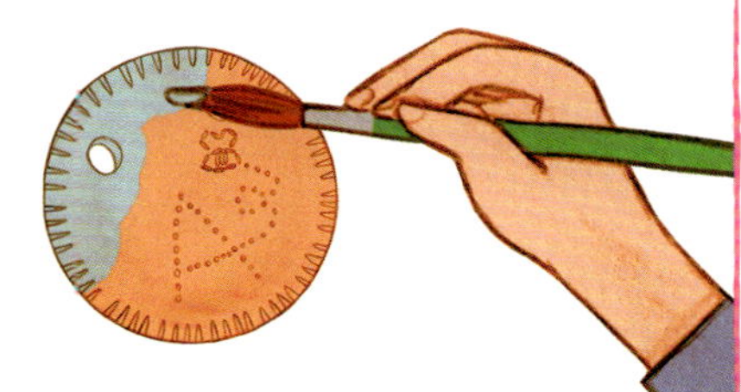

12 Once the clay has dried, use your paintbrush to mix a little blue and white paint together to make a light blue colour. Paint the entire disc with the light-blue paint, then leave to dry.

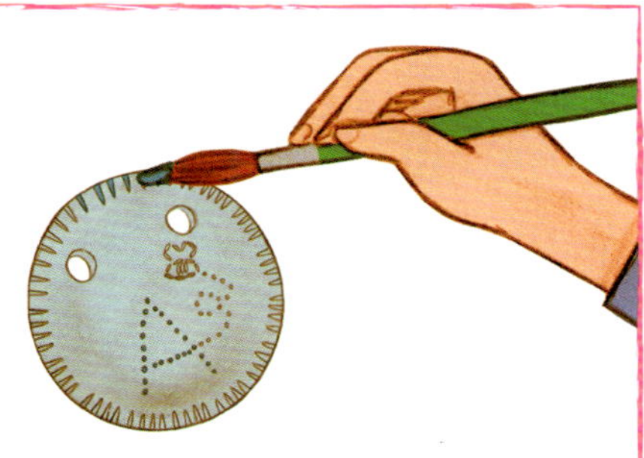

13 Give your paintbrush a wash and a wipe, then dip it in some blue paint. Carefully dab the end of the paintbrush over the toothpick dots and indentations around the edge of the disc.

14 Once the paint has dried, thread the ribbon through the holes and tie a knot either side to hold it in place.

Pom-pom garland

You will need:

A mug
(with an 8cm base)

1 small piece
of cardboard
(about 20cm x 20cm)

A pencil

Scissors

A ball of wool

Pom-poms are used for so many crafts. Whether they're added to the top of a knitted hat, the end of a keyring or even a crafty collage, these fluffy creations look amazing. Make as many pom-poms as you like, fasten them to a length of wool and hang them in your room.

Method:

1 Place your mug on the cardboard and use your pencil to draw around the base. Cut out the circle, using your scissors.

2 Repeat step 1 so that you have 2 cut-out cardboard discs.

3 Ask an adult to help you wiggle your pencil into the middle of each disc to make a small hole. Then use scissors to make a bigger hole (about 2cm wide) in the centre of each disc.

4 Cut away a 2m length of wool from the ball.

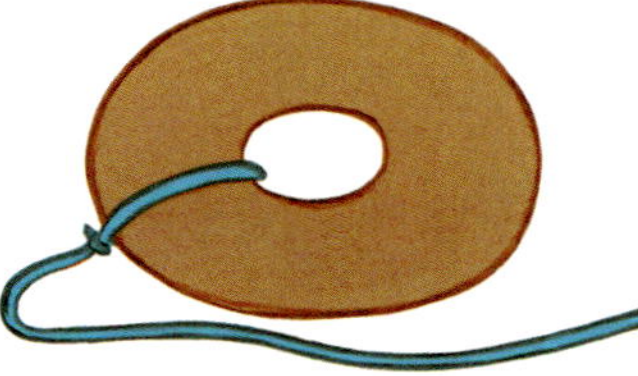

5 Put the doughnut-shaped discs on top of each other, making sure the holes align. Loop the wool through the hole and back around the discs. Where the wool meets, tie a knot to fasten in place.

6 Continue to loop the wool through the hole and around the edge of the discs, weaving the wool around until the entire doughnut shape is covered.

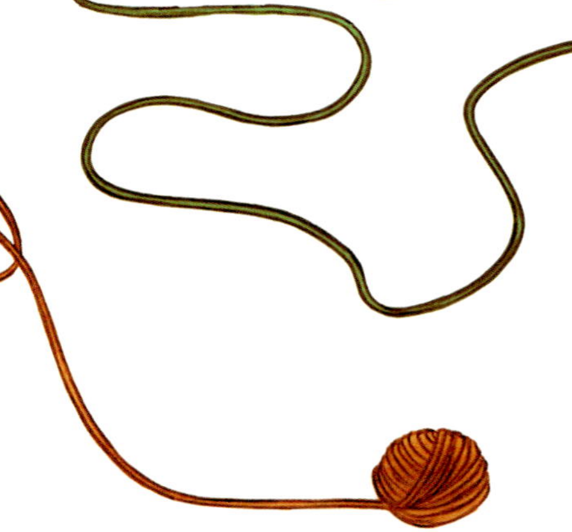

Crafty tip:

Use different colours of wool for each pom-pom to make a multicoloured garland.

7 Once your doughnut is full, tie a little knot in the wool and snip away any excess.

8 Ask your adult to help you wiggle your scissors into the outer edge of the wool. Snip around the outside of the woven disc to release strands of wool.

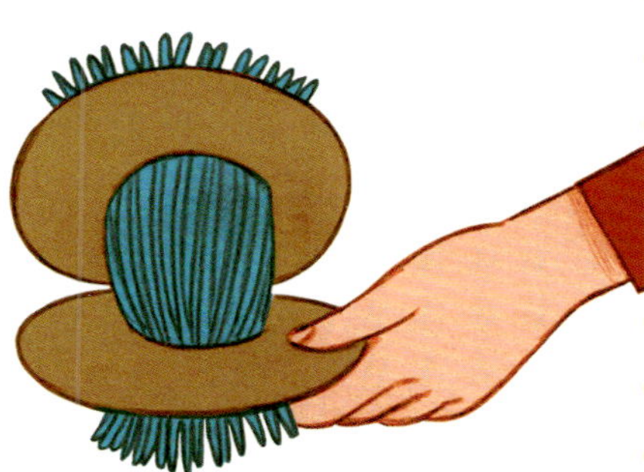

9 Flip the doughnut shape on its side and start to wiggle the cardboard discs apart, being careful not to completely slip the discs off the wool.

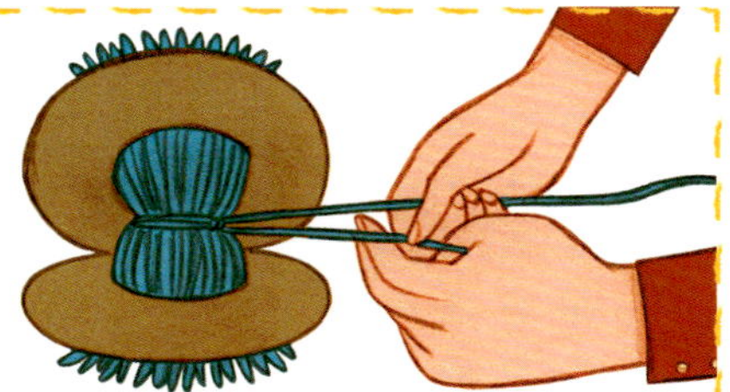

10 Cut away a 10cm length of wool from the ball and use it to tie the middle of the bunches of wool between the cardboard discs, leaving a little extra wool trailing away from the pom-pom.

11 Remove the cardboard discs, then use your fingers to fluff out the pom-pom.

12 Repeat steps 4–11 (using your cardboard discs) to make 10 pom-poms.

13 Once you've made your pom-poms, use the little extra trails of wool to fasten them to a long length of wool to create a garland.

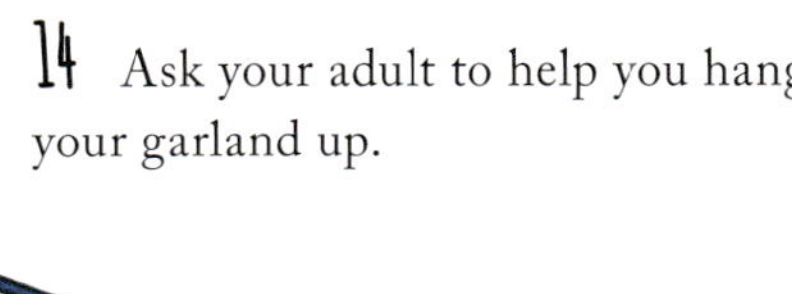

14 Ask your adult to help you hang your garland up.

Cardboard letter light

You will need:

A cardboard box (with a side panel that is at least 40cm x 40cm)

Scissors

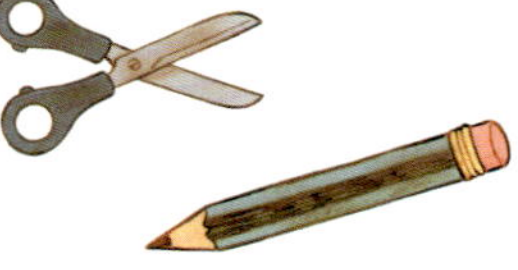

A pencil

A ruler

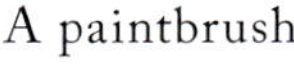

A paintbrush

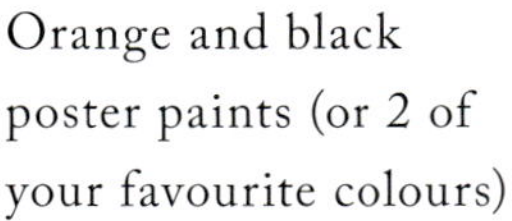

Orange and black poster paints (or 2 of your favourite colours)

A roll of corrugated cardboard

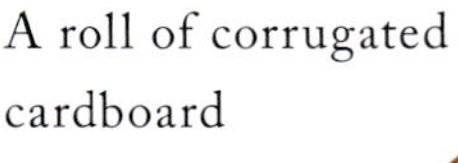

A roll of masking tape

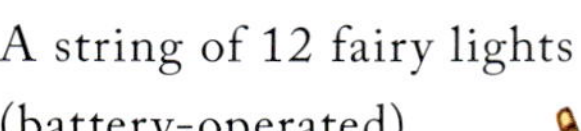

A string of 12 fairy lights (battery-operated)

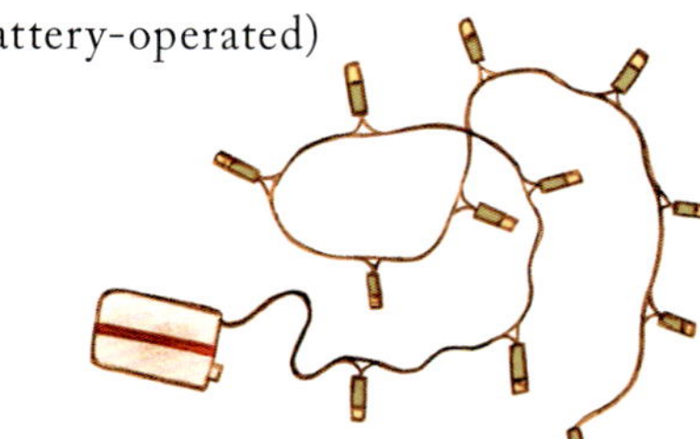

Crafty tip:

If you don't have any corrugated cardboard, stick together smaller scraps of cardboard to make the outer panels of the letter.

Make your room glow with this cardboard letter light that is lightweight as well as bright. For this activity, we are going to make an "A" shape from a leftover cardboard box. If you would like to make a different letter, ask an adult to help you draw one that is roughly the same measurements as the instructions below.

Method:

1 Take your large cardboard box and flatten it. Ask an adult to help you cut out a 40cm x 40cm square from one of the panels.

2 Use your pencil and ruler to draw a (capital) letter "A" on your cardboard, making sure that the bottom and top of the letter fill the cardboard square.

3 Ask your adult to help you cut around the edges of the letter, making sure to get the edges as neat as possible.

4 Paint one side of your letter with orange poster paint, then leave to dry.

5 Flip the letter over so that the painted side is on the bottom. Use your pencil to mark 12 little dots around your letter shape, making them as evenly spaced as you can.

6 Ask your adult to wiggle scissors through each dot, to make small holes. Flip the letter back over so that the painted side is facing you.

7 Roll out the corrugated cardboard. Ask your adult to help you measure 6cm up, then cut out a long length of corrugated card that is 6cm wide.

8 Starting at the side of the letter, line the edge of your corrugated card along the painted side of the letter, making sure the bumpy side of card is facing in and the smooth side is facing out.

9 Flip the letter shape around and stick the corrugated cardboard in place with some masking tape, from the smooth side of the card down to the unpainted side of the letter shape.

10 Cut more 6cm-wide strips of card if you need to, then keep working the cardboard around the letter, stopping at intervals to stick it in place. When you are back where you began, trim away any excess.

11 Once you're happy that the cardboard is securely fastened, paint the masking-taped sides of the corrugated card with black poster paint and leave it to dry.

12 Take your length of fairy lights and space them out. There should be 12 little lights in total.

13 Turn the cardboard letter over, then gently wiggle a fairy light through each hole. Make sure you start at the end of the string of lights, weave around the "A" shape, then put the last light in the centre of the "A".

14 Use the rest of your tape to stick the wires as neatly as you can to the back of the letter. Turn the letter back over, switch on the lights and let it glow!

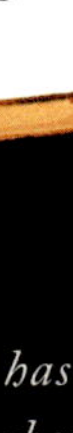

Crafty tip:

Corrugated cardboard has grooves in it, which makes it easier to bend.

THE REPAIR SHOP

Nestled in a beautiful corner of the South Downs lies a very special workshop: The Repair Shop. Inside, Jay Blades and a team of Britain's most skilled craftspeople fix items their owners thought were beyond saving. Every object is a much-loved but broken treasure and, as it is brought back to life, the team finds out the personal story behind it, restoring the memories associated with each object. Since it first appeared on television in 2017, The Repair Shop has fixed hundreds of items. From reviving one of the world's smallest bikes to restoring one of the largest (a derelict penny-farthing), no job is too small or too big for the team.

Sònia Albert graduated from the Children's Book Illustration MA course at the Cambridge School of Art in 2020. She specializes in printmaking, traditional art and digital art, experimenting with different media. Sònia loves to draw with pencils while colouring her drawings digitally, merging them with printmaking textures. She illustrates children's books creating charming characters. In 2020, Sònia was shortlisted for the Sebastian Walker Award. Find out more at www.sonialbert.com